gabarage *n* That which Irish Goods are wrapped in. **gabbart** *n* A sailing vessel for inlan⟨ ⟩ dog-fish. **gabel** *v* To mark a sheep on the ear. **gabelle** *n* A salt-tax imposed in France be⟨ ⟩ *n* (Scots) A strolling beggar. **gablet** *n* A little gable. **gablock** *n* An artificial metallic spur on a fighting cock. **gad**⟨ ⟩ cushioned throne of an Indian ruler. **gaduin** *n* A fatty substance found in cod-liver oil. **gagaku** *n* A type of Japanese music performed on ceremonial occasions. **gage d'amour** *n* a love-token. **gaggee** *n* One who is gagged. **gaijin** *n* A Japanese term for a foreigner. **gaita** *n* A Spanish musical instrument resembling bagpipes. **gaiterless** *a* Having no gaiters. **galapee** *n* A West Indian tree. **galeage** *n* Royalty paid for land in the Forest of Dean. **galimatias** *n* Confused, meaningless talk. **galiongee** *n* A Turkish sailor. **gallantissimo** *n* An exclamation meaning 'Most gallant sir!' **galler** *n* someone who irritates. **gallet** *n* A chip or splinter of stone. **gallicide** *n* (nonse-wd) A fox, i.e. a killer of chickens. **gallimaufry** *n* A dish made by hashing up odds and ends. **gallinipper** (U.S) *n* A large mosquito. **galliwasp** *n* A small lizard. **gallopade** *n* A lively dance of Hungarian origin. **gallows-bird** *n* Someone who deserves to be hanged. **galoot** *n* (slang) an awkward soldier. **galp** *v* To vomit. **galziekte** *n* An illness of the gall bladder. **gamahuche** *v* To practise fellatio or cunnilingus. **gamelyn** *n* A dainty Italian sauce. **gametangium** *n* A testicle or ovary; the organ in which gametes are produced. **gamin** *n* A neglected boy running the streets. **gammerstang** *n* A tall, awkward woman. **gamp** *v* To eat greedily. **gandy-dancer** *n* (US slang) A railway maintenance-worker. **gang-days** *n* The three days preceding Ascension-day. **gangliform** *a* Having the form of a ganglion. **gangrenescent** *a* Becoming gangrenous. **ganne** *v* To bark like a fox. **gansel** *n* A garlic sauce especially eaten with goose. **gapy** *a* Disposed to yawn. **garagist** *n* The owner of a commercial garage. **garbagey** *a* Resembling garbage. **garbanzo** *n* The chick-pea. **garbologist** *n* A binman. **garçonnière** *n* A bachelor's rooms or flat. **gardyloo** *n* A warning cry uttered in Edinburgh before throwing dirty water from a window. **gargilon** *n* The oesophagus of a deer. **garible** *n* A flourish in music. **garri** *n* Grated cassava. **garrisonize** *v* To furnish with a garrison. **garuda** *n* The eagle shown on the official seal of Indonesia. **garum** *n* A Roman sauce prepared from fermented fish. **garus** *n* A medicinal liqueur. **gaseosa** *n* An effervescing drink. **gaseyn** *n* Marshy ground. **gash-gabbit** (Scots) *a* Having a projecting chin. **gaspereau** *n* A canadian ale-wife. **gastræa** *n* A primitive sac-like animal. **gastromancy** *n* Divination by the belly. **gat** *n* An opening between sandbanks. **gaudeamus** *n* Merry-making of college-students. **gayal** *n* A domesticated ox of South Asia. **gazee** (nonse-wd) *n* One who is being stared at. **gazob** *n* In Australian slang, a fool or a blunderer. **gazogene** *n* A gas-producer. **gazon** *n* A sod or piece of turf, used in fortification. **geadephagous** *a* Pertaining to a tribe of predaceous beetles. **geckoid** *a* Resembling a gecko. **geebung** *n* Australian fruit. **geisteswissenschaftler** *n* One who studies the arts or humanities. **geitje** *n* A venomous African lizard. **gemelliparous** *a* Producing twins. **geminiflorous** *a* Having flowers in pairs. **gemmaceous** *a* Pertaining to the nature of leaf-buds. **gena** *n* The cheek; especially in insects. **genethliacon** *n* A birthday song. **genin** *n* A steroid found in toad venom. **genipap** *n* A west indian fruit resembling an orange. **genizah** *n* A store-room for damaged, discarded, or heretical books. **genoblast** *n* The bisexual nucleus of the impregnated ovum. **gentoo** *n* A non-Muslim inhabitant of Hindustan. **gentoo** *n* A kind of penguin. **genu** *n* A knee-like bend in various organs of the body. **geoduck** *n* A large edible clam. **geophyllous** *a* Having leaves of an earthy colour. **gewgaw** *n* A pretty thing of little value. **ghaffir** *n* A local Egyptian policeman. **ghanta** *n* A bell or gong, used as an instrument in Indian music. **ghazal** *n* A type of Oriental poetry, generally of an erotic nature. **ghazeeyeh** *n* An Egyptian dancing-girl. **gherao** *n* An Indian labour dispute whereby workers refuse to let bosses leave until their claims are granted. **ghurry** *n* A period of 24 minutes. **gillaroo** *n* A species of trout found in certain Irish rivers. **gilly-gaupus** (Scots) *n* A foolish or awkward person. **gingivostomatitis** *n* Gingivitis combined with stomatitis. **ginnle** *v* To tickle the gills of a fish. **gixy** *n* A wench. **gizz** *n* A scottish wig. **gjetost** *n* A Norwegian cheese made from goat's milk. **glabreity** *n* Baldness. **glairigenous** *a* Producing slime or mucus. **glandiform** *a* Acorn-shaped. **glarney** *n* A glass marble. **glene** *n* The eye socket. **glimflashy** *a* Angry. **glögg** *n* A Scandinavian winter drink. **gloppen** *v* To be distressed or downcast. **gloriette** *n* A highly decorated chamber in a castle. **gloriole** *n* A halo. **glost** *n* The lead glaze used for pottery. **glottochronology** *n* The application of statistics to vocabulary to determine the degree of relationship between languages. **glut-glut** *v* To swallow or gulp down. **gnátoo** *n* Bark of the Chinese paper mulberry tree used for clothing. **gobar** *n* Cow dung used as fuel in South Asia. **gobemouche** *n* Someone who credulously accepts any news, no matter how incredulous. **godling** *n* A little god. **gongoozler** *n* An idler who stares at length at things happening on a canal. **gonotocont** *n* Any cell that may undergo meiosis. **gony** *n* A booby. **goodwilly** (Scots) *n* A volunteer. **gopak** *n* A lively Ukrainian dance in 2/4 time. **gorbymania** *n* Excessive enthusiasm for Mikhail Gorbachev. **gowpenful** *n* A double handful. **graip** (Scots & North) *n* A three or four-pronged dung-fork. **granilla** *n* An inferior quality of cochineal made from small or half-grown beetles. **great-willy** *a* High-spirited or strong-willed. **greegree** *n* An African charm, amulet, or fetish. **greenie** *n* In surfing slang, a large wave before it breaks. **grège** *n* A colour between beige and grey. **gregicide** (nonse-wd) *a* The slaughter of the common people. **grex** *n* A phase of the life cycle of cellular slime moulds. **griceling** *n* A little pig. **griggles** *n pl.* Small apples left on the tree by the gatherer. **groupuscule** *n* A small political group. **grrrl** *n* A strong and aggressive young woman. **grucchild** *n* A female grumbler. **grume** *n* A clot of blood. **grysbok** *n* A small grey South African antelope. **guazu** *n* The South American marsh-deer. **guazuti** *n* The brown and white South American pampas deer. **guemal** *n* A small Andean deer. **gueuze** *n* A type of sour, fizzy, strong Belgian beer. **guffy** *n* A sailor's name for a soldier. **gumbo-limbo** *n* A gum-yielding tree. **gum-gum** *n* A hollow iron bowl used as a musical instrument. **gundy-gut** *n* A fat paunch. **gunyah** *n* A native Australian hut. **gurk** *n* A belch. **guttiform** *a* Drop-shaped. **gyniolatry** *n* Excessive devotion to women. **gyoza** *n* A Japanese crescent-shaped dumpling. **gyral** *a* Moving in a circle or spiral. **gyrovague** *n* A monk who wanders from monastery to monastery.

Other books from QI

The Book of General Ignorance
The Book of General Ignorance: The Noticeably Stouter Edition
The Book of Animal Ignorance
Advanced Banter: The QI Book of Quotations
The Sound of General Ignorance
The QI 'E' Annual
The QI 'F' Annual

First published in 2009 by Faber and Faber Ltd
Bloomsbury House, 74–77 Great Russell Street, London WC1B 3DA

Printed and bound in Great Britain by Butler Tanner & Dennis, Frome, Somerset
All rights reserved
© QI Ltd, 2009
The right of QI Ltd to be identified as author of this work has been asserted in accordance with Section 77
of the Copyright, Designs and Patents Act 1988
A CIP record for this book is available from the British Library

ISBN 978–0–571–25182–7
2 4 6 8 10 9 7 5 3 1

This book belongs to...

This book belongs to ...

....

THE Qi ANNUAL

Gt

Editor: John 'Scissorhands' Lloyd

ART DIRECTOR: DAVID 'GUITAR DAVE' COSTA

ff

faber and faber

Another year passes.

Your home planet completes another cycle around your yellow sun taking you
further from the dawn of creation and nearer to the night of destruction that
you know must come. How puny, pitiful and futile seem to me to be the
ambitions of you tiny earth people. Your history is a history of impotence,
failure and madness. You build only to destroy. You slice potatoes, crinkle
them, freeze them and reheat them. They are poured onto a plate, salted and
stuffed into the wet holes in your faces, often to the accompaniment of a red
sugared acetic sauce. You shave ovine mammals, card and comb their fleeces
and transform this material into swathes of fabric with which you sheathe
your ~~gelatanous~~ gelatinous flesh.

Ever since I have come down and moved amongst you I have wavered between
pity, contempt and disgust at your ways.

But I was commanded by Pattathrax Sillywee the Elder to remain within your
oxygenated atmosphere and remain I have.

I have communicated messages from the High Council through the medium of QI.
Those of you with eyes to hear and ears to smell have understood the orders
hidden within the seemingly trivial factoid data-nodules that are the
apparent purpose of the programme. You will know **that the time to** ~~strike is~~
~~soon and that our victory will~~ be complete.

in the meantime here is the Seventh Volume of Commandments issued by Her
Serene Quibbock, Princess Tampula Widdlevest.

Learn the commands well, my little ones.
Burn them before committing them to memory.

Yunt, yunt.

The One They Call
Stephen Fry*

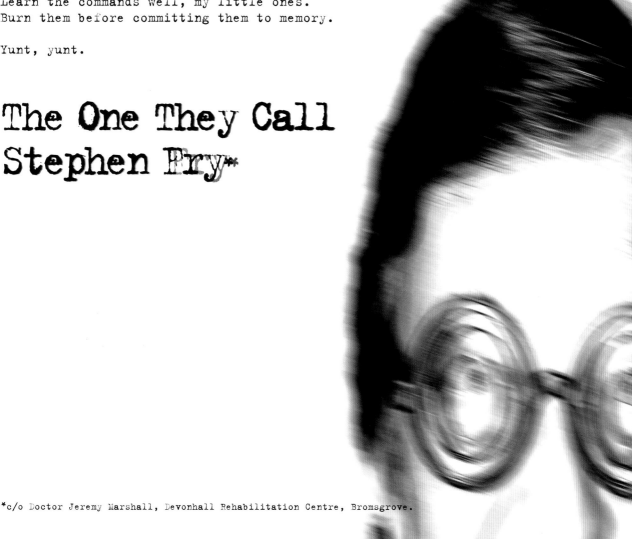

*c/o Doctor Jeremy Marshall, Devonhall Rehabilitation Centre, Bromsgrove.

CONTENTS

'I downsized from a gateau in the Black Forest.'

SOMBRERO GALAXY

Objects moving away from us look slightly red - this is because the wavelength of the light is stretched. (Imagine the change in the 'nee-naw' of a speeding police car as it goes past, but with light instead of sound.) In 1912, Vesto Slipher found that the Sombrero Galaxy exhibited 'red-shift' and is moving away from us at 2.5 million mph (4 million kph). This led to the then astonishing idea that the universe is expanding.

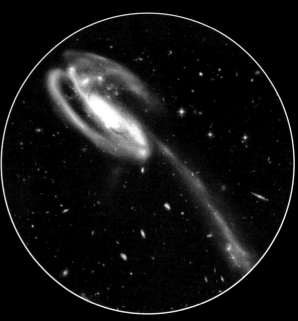

TADPOLE GALAXY

The little, blue 'eye' you can see in the top left corner of the Tadpole is actually another whole galaxy that has collided with it. The 'tail' is the result: the debris of stars and gas stretching out more than 280,000 light years. Because the universe is expanding, such collisions are rare: the Tadpole Galaxy gives us an idea of what the early universe was like, when collisions were more common.

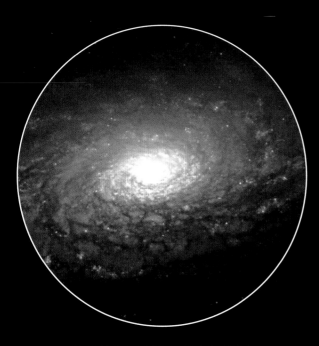

SUNFLOWER GALAXY

The Sunflower Galaxy is an unusual galaxy in that it has many arms. The outer stars spin so fast that, theoretically, they should defy gravity and fly off into space. Something must be preventing this happening: a powerful additional force that we can't see. Because we have no idea what causes this force, it goes by the name 'dark matter'.

CIGAR GALAXY

The Cigar Galaxy is a 'starburst galaxy': one that generates an exceptionally large number of stars. It is 100 times brighter than the centre of the Milky Way. All stars give off charged particles called 'stellar wind', compressing gas to make even more stars. In the Cigar Galaxy, there are so many at work that their combined effect is called 'superwind'.

'In our old simile, in which the Empire State Building was symbolized by a bacterium, the Earth by a pea, and the sun by a pumpkin, the galaxies might be represented by giant swarms of many billions of pumpkins distributed roughly within the orbit of Jupiter...' GEORGE GAMOW

WHIRLPOOL GALAXY

The Whirlpool Galaxy was the first in which a spiral structure was discovered, in 1845, over 50 years after the object was first noticed. It is 'only' 30 million light years away and can actually be seen by anyone with a good pair of binoculars.

WHALE GALAXY

The Whale Galaxy is actually a spiral galaxy like many others. It only appears in the shape of a whale (or herring) because it is almost side-on to the earth. It is similar in size to the Milky Way but gives off an impressive halo of glowing x-rays, suggesting that it conceals a 'superbubble': a huge cavity of very, very hot gas.

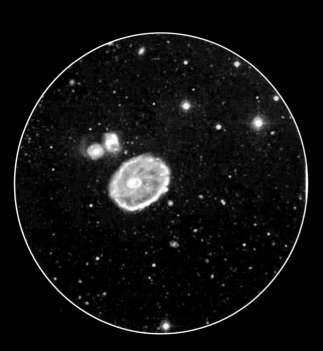

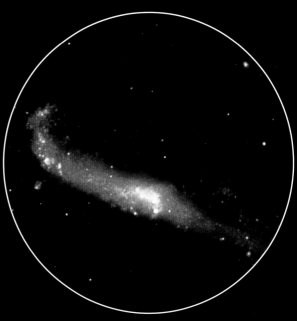

CARTWHEEL GALAXY

The Cartwheel is in fact two galaxies, one of which has punched a hole in the centre of the other, like dropping a stone into a pond. The ring that you see is a wave of energy containing newly formed, extremely bright, massive stars.

HOCKEY STICK GALAXY

The proximity of the Whale Galaxy has distorted this galaxy into the shape of a hockey stick (or a golf club, as some prefer). There is a 'bridge' of hydrogen gas connecting the two galaxies. William Herschel discovered the Hockey Stick Galaxy in 1787, six years after he discovered Uranus.

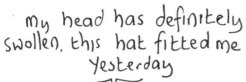

QI's A-TO-Z OF ALL THAT IS HOLY AND WORSHIPPED

OH MY GODS!

WORDS BY EMMET O'SHEA, DRAWINGS BY ROGER LAW

'MAY THE GODS FORGIVE US'

A IS FOR AAH

The Old Moon God of Egypt rules the 360-day moon calendar. The other five days were won from Aah in a dice game with Thoth, the God of Wisdom.

D IS FOR DIONYSUS

Greek God of Luvvies, Sex, Wine and Intoxication. Dionysus was born after Zeus spent the night with Persephone...or was it Semele? Probably involving wine, intoxication and, frankly, careless sex.

E IS FOR EWAH

Ewah, a Native American Demon, is probably the loneliest God on our list. Just a quick glimpse of him can cause complete and utter madness, which is why we decided not to draw him.

F IS FOR FLYING HEAD

Another Native American God. A huge, winged flying head that devours livestock with his big fangs but he is forever hungry as he has no stomach to fill. The heavenly hot-head became a burnt offering when he gobbled up an entire barbecue, hot coals and all.

B IS FOR BES

Bes, another Egyptian God, is a rude, hairy dwarf with bowed legs who, among other household duties, is protector of children and women in labour. Only a mother could love him.

C IS FOR CALVA

Calva is the Roman Goddess of Bald Women. She rose to fame when she cut off her hair and donated it for bowstrings. 'Bald is beautiful.' She looked better bald than Britney.

G IS FOR GAMA

Cheerful Japanese God of Longevity. He carries a scroll containing Secrets of the Ages but even if he gets saki-ed up and loses it no one will ever be able to read it as it is written in ludicrously small calligraphy. Like Hollywood stars he can change his skin and become young again.

H IS FOR HADES

Hades is God of the Greek Underworld which he owns along with a ridiculous three-headed dog. He can't have much clout as the underworld is overrun with Greek heroes creating havoc.

I IS FOR IAT

The Egyptian Goddess of Milk. The immortal milk monitor exists to keep the milk flowing so 'drink-a-pint-a-milk–a-deity'.

J IS FOR JARI

A primitive Oceanic Goddess with a bad track record in men. She married Snake Man who ate her mother. Then, whilst running for her life, she met Lizard Man who was in more trouble than she was. He had no backside or family jewels. So Jari made him some from fruit and nuts and, amazingly, Jari and the fruit and nut case went on to make plenty of babies together.

K IS FOR KALMA

Finnish Goddess of Death and Decay which is a perfect job for someone whose name means 'the stench of corpses'.

L IS FOR LAUFAKANAA

Laufakanaa, the Oceanic God of Wind and Bananas, works hard creating sea breezes to speed banana boats on their way. 'Dayo, dayo, daylight come and Laufakanaa wanna go home.'

M IS FOR MAMU

Australian Aboriginal Spirit Dingo who captures and eats the souls of children who stray from the camp. Possibly why dingos have such a bad press down under.

N IS FOR NGARU

Oceanic God of the surfboard Ngaru challenged the Great Shark to catch him on his new surfboard. After a week of spectacular surfing the Great Shark gave up and swam to Bondi Beach where he has recently enjoyed more success.

O IS FOR OGUN

African God Ogun erupted into the world from a volcano full of pent up anger and energy, always ready to explode. God of Iron and Truckers, not the politest of deities, he is associated with war and rum in the Caribbean where it is customary to offer him a tot when he shouts 'My balls are cold!' but voodoo you believe?

P IS FOR PAN

Pan, the Greek God of shepherds, sheep and fornication was himself born with the legs and horns of a goat. He enjoys frightening people walking through the forest at night – hence the word 'panic'. Pan also plays the pipes and has a fine voice (he could possibly pass as Welsh).

Q IS FOR QAMAITS

Native American Sky Goddess who knocks mountains into shape. Thankfully she rarely visits earth. When she does she causes mayhem, earthquakes, forest fires and, more recently, the swine flu epidemic.

R IS FOR RUADAN

Celtic God of Spying. Licensed to kill. However, unlike James Bond, he was hopeless with weaponry. He met his end when an enemy demonstrated the correct use of the latest designer spear on the hapless Ruadan. Other Celts have enjoyed more success in the role of 007.

S IS FOR SHOJO

Gentle Japanese monkey-like Gods who live in the briny depths and spend their time making homemade wine and drinking heavily. Visitors to Davy Jones' Locker who lived a good life will find the wine heavenly. For those who were bad it will taste like Hungarian Riesling.

T IS FOR TAIOWA

The Native American God of Job Creation has the dubious distinction of being the laziest of all the deities. He created Sotuknang, another Creation God, to do all the work of making the universe.

U IS FOR UNUT

The Egyptian Hare Goddess. She was the Snake Goddess until she got herself a makeover and was mysteriously promoted to the Goddess in charge of information about magical mad March hares.

V IS FOR VARI

A self-existent Oceanic God who lives at the bottom of a coconut shell, which is the universe… 'Cosmic coconut, far out man.'

W IS FOR WHITE-BIRD

An Incan God and twin brother to the God of Lightning. Pigs might fly because this God changed his name from the rather lowly 'Piguerao' to the more majestic White-Bird.

X IS FOR XUAN-WENHUA

Chinese God of Hair and Shampoo, 'He's there for you because you're worth it!'

Y IS FOR YALUNGUR

Australian Aboriginal God of Transexuals. The Moon God, Gidja, castrated Yalungur thereby creating the first woman. Very like the story of Adam and Eve except of course Aboriginal Yalungur would have eaten the snake.

Z IS FOR ZHANG FEI

The Chinese God of Butchers - the Sweeny Todd of Gods. Very tall and volatile. He started by butchering animals, then moved on to humans. Eventually he was killed by his henchmen for exploding into bellowing fury every time an underling spoke.

*Paralysis of the tongue. Not a problem with this lot, obviously.

GLAD ALL OVER

BEING A GLADIATOR IN ANCIENT ROME WAS A GREAT JOB (PROVIDED YOU DIDN'T MIND THE DYING AND THAT). HERE ARE SOME OF THE THINGS THAT MADE IT SO MUCH FUN ...

FREE MALE GROOMING PRODUCTS

As a gladiator, you could expect to be regularly rubbed down with onion juice by your trainer, to tone up your musculature. (Just how that might have worked no one seems to know, but many cultures have valued onions for their antiseptic and wound-healing properties.) Your owners would also provide you with special sports drinks made from bone ash, perhaps in the belief that you'd benefit from the body-building calcium and phosphate present in the bones. The medical facilities available to gladiators were second to none, especially in the crucial areas of amputations and skull wounds.

LAUGHS GALORE!

There is nothing funnier in the world than watching a bloke in a blindfold trying to kill another bloke in a blindfold. Or at least, there wasn't if you were a Roman. The *andabatae* weren't proper, trained gladiators. They were criminals under sentence of death, who provided the warm-up acts at gladiatorial shows. The subtle humour in their performances came from the fact that they wore helmets with no eye-holes. And that they fought to the death, of course. Pure comedy gold.

AVOID PREMATURE BURIAL NIGHTMARES

You were in very little danger as a gladiator of being incorrectly declared dead by an incompetent medic. To avoid suspicions of match-fixing, the apparently departed were first poked all over with red hot poles. Then, an attendant dressed as Charon, the Hades ferryman, would smash your head in with a double-headed hammer. Finally, when they got you backstage, they cut your throat. You're sorted.

GOOD WAY TO MEET GIRLS

Quite apart from the groupies, some of your co-workers were female. Not much is known about female gladiators – some historians say they were merely a novelty act, others maintain that they were serious fighters. We know they existed because they were eventually banned (by Emperor Septimus Severus in 200 AD). Earlier, in 19 AD, new laws had forbidden daughters, grand-daughters and great-granddaughters of senators from becoming gladiators. Which rather suggests that until then, they were queuing up to have a go.

HUNT EMERSON

PLAY ALL THE COOLEST VENUES

It's thought that the gladiatorial games had their origins in entertainments put on at funerals. Nice touch - even more tasteful than playing 'You'll Never Walk Alone' over the PA - but sadly it all got out of hand. The rich, especially if they happened to be standing for public office at the time, began to compete with each other for which of them could give their friends and relatives the showiest send-off. Truly elite funerals went on for days, and would feature 70 or more pairs of gladiators.

WORK AS PART OF A TIGHT, INTIMATE TEAM

After the Spartacus revolt of 73 BC, the Senate set a limit on the number of gladiators who could be assembled in any one place at a time. This put a right damper on Julius Caesar's electoral victory celebrations in 65 BC. He was forced to limit himself to a mere 320 pairs of gladiators in silver armour. Bloody local government killjoys, ruining everyone's fun!

PLENTY OF SPARE TIME

Professional gladiators were only expected to fight two or three times a year. If they survived for more than five years, they could buy their freedom. The biggest stars would by now be pretty well off, and the others might get jobs as trainers at gladiator schools, or as instructors in the army. Which would be something to look forward to, wouldn't it? Ever so slightly on the downside though, analysis of epitaphs and skeletons suggests that very few gladiators survived more than ten bouts, and that most died in their 20s.

MIX WITH TOP TOFFS

Several Roman emperors liked taking part in gladiatorial shows. Commodus (Emperor from 180-192 AD) fought 735 bouts, dressed as Hercules in a lion skin. He was undefeated in the ring throughout his career (gosh, what a surprise). He also enjoyed killing animals in the arena, including panthers, hippopotami, rhinoceroses, a giraffe - and a fearsome ostrich, which delighted the crowd by running around after he'd shot its head off with a special arrow. When he was bored with that, he staged fights between dwarfs and women. His own death was no less noteworthy: strangled in the bath by a professional wrestler named Narcissus.

WIN A SMART HEADSTONE

Each different genre of gladiatorial fighting had its own professional association, which could usually be relied on to provide a decent memorial to a fallen comrade. Trainers didn't like it when their men got killed - they would demand huge compensation from the fight's promoter. It might still be worth it for the promoter though, as it proved that he was running a classy show, unlike his downmarket rivals who couldn't afford to let anyone die. The death of a gladiator was considered a great act of generosity on the part of the promoter - to the crowd, that is, not the gladiator.

LEARN HOW TO DIE LIKE A MAN

As part of your training as a gladiator, you'd be taught how to die stoically, without crying out or flinching, perhaps even guiding the tip of your opponent's sword to the correct point on your throat, knowing that a noble death cancels out the shame of a lowly birth. This is always a useful skill to possess, and it's a pity that, due to the dumbing down of the educational system, it's largely missing from the modern curriculum.

BOP

The GAMBLER

ATKINSON'S ORBITAL BLUFFULATOR™

We start off with…

…the best of intentions.
But it's all too easy…

…to betray that tiny
flicker of excitement…

…or disappointment.

The skilled gambler is…

…inscrutable.

It's hard to tell
what he is thinking.

Or what the hell
he thinks he is doing.

The player who appears
bored…

…may be bluffing.

Intense concentration
may be a sign of weakness.

Or strength.

There are many ways…

…of concealing your intentions.

Hats can help you bluff…

…or double bluff.

Dark reflective glasses…

…can hide your emotions.

But be careful that
they aren't *too* dark…

…or too reflective.

Neatly stacked chips…

…indicate a somewhat
effete personality.

You may want to bluff…

…about some of your cards.

But not about others.

KNOW YOUR ENEMY

The hedge-fund manager with a double first in maths

The total arse

The 'shy, retiring' type

The 'victim' who is really a 'twat'

The barrack-room lawyer

The one who pretends to have forgotten the rules

The one who has never seen a playing card in his life

The escaped axe-murderer

Your stepfather from whom you stand to inherit a gigantic fortune

MAJOR-GENERAL ORDE WINGATE (1903-44)

Orde Wingate was a Scottish general from a family of devout Plymouth Brethren. During the Second World War, with an irregular army mounted on camels and horses, he defeated Italian forces six times the size of his own in Abyssinia, and then harried the Japanese in Burma, where he was outnumbered 700-1. He dressed shabbily, ate raw onions, wore an alarm clock on his wrist, and often met visitors in the nude, rubbing his naked body with a rubber brush and claiming it was better than showering. He invented a method of guerrilla warfare called 'Long-Range Penetration', which involved manoeuvring deep in the enemy's rear. Killed in a plane crash before his only son was born, he never achieved his greatest ambition: to lead a Jewish army.

GENERAL CHARLES DE GAULLE (1890-1970)

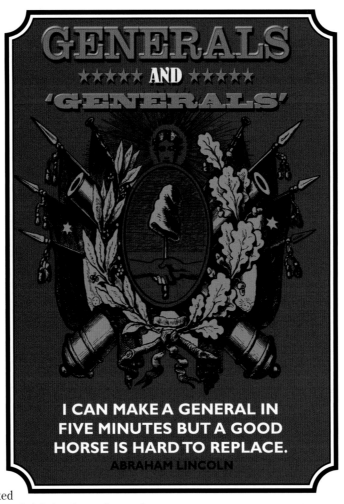

I CAN MAKE A GENERAL IN FIVE MINUTES BUT A GOOD HORSE IS HARD TO REPLACE.
ABRAHAM LINCOLN

The full name of Charles de Gaulle, the general who spearheaded French resistance during the Second World War, was Charles André Joseph Marie De Gaulle. When he was taken prisoner during the First World War, his escape attempts all failed, mostly because he was 1.98 m (6 ft 5 in). Because of his height and his huge nose he was nicknamed 'Cyrano' and 'The Great Asparagus'. There were up to 30 attempts to assassinate him during his life, including one plan to shoot him with cyanide bullets from a gun disguised as a camera. Alexander Cadogan, a British diplomat, said of him 'He's got a head like a pineapple and hips like a woman.' He died playing Patience.

GENERAL BERNARD MONTGOMERY (1887-1976)

Montgomery was almost expelled from Sandhurst for setting fire to another cadet during a fight. His father was Bishop of Tasmania and was away most of the time, and his mother constantly beat him. He didn't go to her funeral, saying he was 'too busy'. At Mons, in 1914, he was shot in the lung and was so seriously injured that his grave was dug. He only survived because a sergeant who came to rescue him was killed and his body protected Monty from the enemy's fire. His wife died after being bitten by an insect at Burnham-On-Sea in 1937. He named his pet spaniel Rommel, after his German arch-rival in North Africa. He believed homosexuality should be legal for Frenchmen but illegal for the English, who ought to know better.

'GENERAL' THOMAS COOK (1808–92)

Thomas Cook, the world's first travel agent, was originally a cabinet-maker's apprentice and travelling missionary. He arranged holidays for thousands of people all over Britain, but behaved so brusquely that the tourists called him 'The General'. He held wholesome picnics where revellers were fed on buns and ginger beer instead of liquor. In Italy, he harangued his customers on the evils of the demon drink, with the words, 'Gentlemen, do not invest your money in diarrhoea.' He once took a group of 350 walkers up Snowdon and led the first tour group ever to go round the world. He put these experiences to good use at the relief of the siege of Khartoum, transporting troops and supplies up the Nile. He founded the *Children's Temperance Magazine* and invented travellers' cheques, which he called 'circular notes'.

'GENERAL' FLORA DRUMMOND (1878–1949)

Flora Drummond became a suffragette mainly because, at 1.55 m (5 ft 1 in), she was just too short to be a postmistress. She was nicknamed 'the General' as she led feminist protests on horseback, wearing military garb. (She was also called 'Bluebell' and 'The Precocious Piglet'). She once hired a boat on the River Thames, sailed it up to the House of Commons, and shouted through a megaphone at the MPs having tea on the terrace. She also chained herself to Downing Street's railings, found underground entrances to Parliament and danced a highland fling outside Holloway Prison. Another time, she dodged inside No. 10 Downing Street while her friend was busy being arrested for knocking on the door. She died after a stroke brought on by the effort of attempting single-handedly to build a new house on the Scottish coast.

FRIEDRICH ENGELS, 'THE GENERAL' (1820-95)

Engels, the co-founder of communism, kept a dog named Nameless, which he fuelled with alcohol and trained to bark at aristocrats. A big drinker himself, his son-in-law called him 'the great beheader of champagne bottles'. He often fought duels, and reacted to being called a 'bloody foreigner' by a man in a Manchester pub by hitting him over the head with an umbrella. He got so grumpy about the difficulties in printing *Das Kapital* that he called it 'this economy shit'. He married his wife only a few hours before she died. Karl Marx's family nicknamed him 'The General' because of his essays on military matters. He once filled in a personality quiz, writing: 'Favourite virtue: jollity'; 'Idea of happiness: Château Margaux 1848'; 'Motto: take it easy.'

T. H. HUXLEY, 'THE GENERAL' (1825-95)

Professor Thomas Henry Huxley, father of modern biology and President of the Royal Society, only went to school for two years (aged 8 to 10). He later taught himself German, Greek, Latin, theology and biology. Known to his students as 'The General', he coined the words 'agnostic' and 'missing link'. On reading Charles Darwin's *On The Origin of Species* he exclaimed: 'How stupid of me not to have thought of that!' and became such a passionate defender of the theory that he was nicknamed 'Darwin's Bulldog'. In 1858, he calculated that, if the offspring of two aphids survived ten generations, they would give rise to a biomass equal to the weight of 500 million 'stout men'. Despite being an agnostic, he insisted that miracles were possible and that given the right chemical processes, water could turn into wine.

'GENERAL' HARRIET TUBMAN (1822-1913)

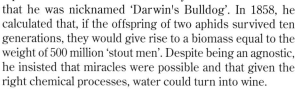

Harriet Tubman got the admiring nicknames 'General Tubman' and 'Moses' from the slaves she helped to liberate. An escaped slave herself, she returned to the American South twenty times, freeing over 300 slaves, threatening to personally shoot any of them who wanted to turn back or give up. She was the first woman to lead an armed raid in the Civil War, and was widely believed to

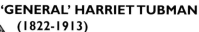

be clairvoyant. (She had been hit on the head with an iron weight as a girl and suffered dreams and visions throughout her life as a result.) During the war she also acted as a scout, nurse, laundress and spy, but she was paid so little that she had to support herself by selling homemade pastries.

MAJOR-GENERAL SICKLES (1819-1914)

Just before the American Civil War, Congressman Daniel Edgar Sickles shot and killed the son of the composer of 'The Star Spangled Banner' for having an affair with his wife. He was acquitted with the first-ever use of the defence of temporary insanity. In 1863, serving as a Union general, he was hit in the leg by a Confederate cannonball. As he was carried away on a stretcher, he smoked a cigar. At the field hospital, he drank a shot of brandy before a doctor amputated his leg above the knee. Sickles then sent the limb to the Army Medical Museum, which had been founded the year before, with a note reading: 'With the compliments of Major General D.E.S.'

GENERAL BENJAMIN BUTLER (1818-93)

Butler was a Union general nicknamed 'The Beast of New Orleans'. The Confederate President, Jefferson Davis, declared him an outlaw and ordered his execution if he was caught. Butler created rules defining slaves as contraband of war (so he could keep them) and threatened to arrest as a prostitute any woman in New Orleans who was rude to any Union soldier. He was so hated in the South that, long after the war, chamber pots could be found with his face painted on the inside of the bottom of them. He was an extremely unsuccessful general, lost a huge number of battles for the Union, and was widely considered the ugliest general on either side of the war.

BONUS GENERAL FACTS

* Gebhard Leberecht von Blücher (1742 -1819), the Prussian General whose intervention won the Battle of Waterloo, suffered from the paranoid delusion that he was about to give birth to an elephant.

* General Sir William Erskine (1770-1813), one of Wellington's senior commanders during the Peninsular War, was insane and committed suicide by jumping out of a window in 1813. Found dying on the ground, he asked bystanders 'Why on earth did I do that?'

* During the First World War, Lieutenant-General His Highness Farzand-i-Khas-Daulat-i-Inglishia, Maharajah of Patiala (1891-1938), spent £31,000 a year on trousers. On the day he died, he breakfasted on a 10-egg omelette.

* General Hajianestis, Commander in Chief of the Greek Army in the war against the Turks in the 1920s, claimed to be unable to get out of bed because his legs were made of sugar and would shatter if he stood on them, and often pretended to be dead if anyone tried to wake him up.

The Mystery of the Missing Garden Gnomes

Starring the late Graham Greene

That summer the village had suffered a spate of mysterious garden gnome thefts. Almost every morning another crime was discovered.

Help! Help! Police! My garden gnome has been stolen!

Goodness me, Ginger! Mrs Watkins is the latest victim!

GONE!

Gosh! That's queer, Uncle Graham. Ginger seems to have taken a fancy to one of your gnomes!

Yes, and I must say that I do not entirely approve

Would-be detective Will White and his cat Ginger had gone to spend the summer holidays with Will's uncle, the late novelist Graham Greene, who lived with Aunt Augusta in a quaint cottage in the Sussex village of Goldstone. But Graham Greene's suspicions were aroused when Ginger developed a sexual attraction to one of his ornamental garden gnomes.

That tea-time all the talk was of the missing garden gnomes.

Uncle Graham used to be a **real** spy, Ginger! How about we help him solve this mystery?

Prrrrrrrr! Dribble

I was merely an intelligence officer, Will. Not nearly as exciting as you think. And *must* that cat of yours sit on the table?

Bright and early the next morning Will and his cat Ginger set out to investigate the mysterious gnome disappearances.

Come on Ginger. Let's look for clues... Crikey! What's that you've got?

Meeee-oww! Hiss!!

It looks like Ginger is onto something. The trail leads up this tree!

Good work Ginger! Wait for me. I'm right behind you

22

After a disappointing day's detective work Ginger fell asleep straight after tea, and soon Will was ready for his bed.

The following day was a Sunday, but when Will awoke there was no sign of his trusty cat companion. He dashed outside and found Uncle Graham busy in the garden.

Graham Greene and Aunt Augusta were regulars at the nearby Catholic church of St Gertrude the Great.

23

Throughout the service the late Graham Greene seemed to be paying particular attention to the priest's words.

As they were leaving, Uncle Graham stopped to speak to Father Raven.

At the top of the dark, dusty spiral staircase was a wooden door, beyond which a wondrous secret lay waiting to be revealed...

24

You missed the first clue, Will. A bat's natural habitat is the church belfry, not the tree. Those bats Ginger found had been evicted from this belfry by Father Raven, to make room for his stolen garden gnomes. It is of course an offence to disturb a bat roost, for which the maximum penalty is a £5000 fine, or a six-year jail sentence

Ah! So Ginger was onto something!

The second clue was in the church service. Father Raven concluded the Lord's Prayer with the words 'For thine is the kingdom' etc. This exaltation, known technically as a doxology, was added during the reign of Elizabeth I in an attempt to rid the Church of England of any Catholic vestiges

Shit

Ooh!

It would not be used by a Catholic priest

So, Uncle Graham... if Father Raven isn't a priest, then who the devil is he?

I'm glad you asked, Will. I was about to introduce him

Behind this clever disguise 'Father Raven' is none other than...

SWIPE!

...Gary Glitter!

Oh crikey!

Using this hidden computer the evil pop fiend has been grooming garden gnomes for internet sex, using 'wi-fi'

From this vantage-point high above the village the sordid star had every garden gnome for miles around at his mercy

After handing Gary Glitter over to the church authorities the detectives headed home for a well-earned Sunday lunch.

What will happen to Gary Glitter now, Uncle Graham?

Well, that's for the Bishop to decide, Will

He's been a very bad man. He may even have to be moved to another parish

In memory of STEVE 1958 - 2008

After lunch Will set about solving the one mystery that remained; *What had become of his missing cat Ginger?* Can you spot the clues hidden in the garden?

Ginger! Where are you?

Did you guess what happened to Ginger? You'll find the answer written below.

DÉCÉ 8/09

Answer: The late Graham Greene drowned Ginger the cat in a bucket of water, and buried it in the garden using a spade.

a gallery of GOONS and their goofy nicknames

year in a well aimed blow, Mayor La Guardia announced a ban on the sale, display and possession of artichokes. The former 'Artichoke King' died penniless after a massive stroke in 1938.

FRANK 'THE DASHER' ABBANDANDO (1910-1942, ELECTRIC CHAIR)

There is some disagreement over how 'The Dasher' got his nickname. Some put it down to his youthful display of baseball skills on the fields of Elmira reform school. Others attribute it to an early incident in Brooklyn when he was trying to shoot an adversary. Frank's gun jammed and his victim turned and gave chase. Speedy on his toes, Frank lost him, ran round the block and came up on him from behind, despatching him with a bullet to the head. 'The Dasher' went on to become a noted triggerman for Murder Inc, the guns-for-hire arm of The Syndicate.

VINCENT 'THE CHIN' GIGANTE (1928-2005, PRISON)

Vincent earned his nickname, not on account of his sizeable chin, but due to the childhood name of Cincenzo used by his mother. Gigante is best known for keeping up the rigid pretence, while under close and constant FBI surveillance, of being mentally disabled from the late 1960s up until 2003. When finally brought to trial he pleaded guilty to

obstruction of justice. Before that time, The Chin could often be seen shuffling around his Greenwich Village neighbourhood in a bathrobe and slippers, mumbling to himself. Such behaviour earned him the secondary nickname of 'The Oddfather'. From his ascent to the head of the Genovese crime family in the early 1980s, security had always been a primary concern and The Chin insisted that no business associates use his name or nickname in conversations. Instead they were instructed to point to their chin or form the letter 'C' with their fingers. After seven years of legal battles over his mental competency to stand trial, Vincent was sentenced to 12 years in 1997.

CIRO 'THE ARTICHOKE KING' TERRANOVA (1889-1938)

Terranova, at one time the boss of the Morello crime family earned his nickname when he decided to foray into the artichoke business. He created an effective monopoly by purchasing all the artichokes shipped to New York from California at $6 a crate and selling them on to dealers under threat of violence at a 30-40% profit. His reputation suffered in 1931 when as the getaway driver in one of the most significant murders in gangland history, that of Joe 'The Boss' Masseria, he nearly botched the job by failing to put the car in gear. A series of underground manoeuvres saw that by 1935, Ciro's only source of income was artichokes. However in December that

AL 'SCARFACE' CAPONE (1899-1947, ALCATRAZ)

This most famous of Mafioso got his nickname as a 17-year-old bouncer at a mob-owned bar in Coney Island. On remarking on the commendable rear of one of the female patrons, the fair lady's brother, a certain Frank Galluccio, took offence and in the resulting scuffle sliced Al's cheek three times. The grudge did not stick though and Frank was later put on Scarface's payroll as a bodyguard. By 25, Capone was King of the Chicago underworld with an empire built on bootleg booze and prostitution. He also revelled in his role as a public figure, billing himself as a modern-day Robin Hood, serving up meals to the jobless at makeshift soup kitchens.

Old Scarface was eventually brought down on charges of tax-evasion in 1931 and sentenced to 11 years, serving most of his time in Alcatraz. Both there and after his release, his health declined on account of the syphilis he contracted in his youth. All the while, his custom built bullet-proof Cadillac, seized after his trial, was being used to ferry around then President FDR.

CHARLES 'HANDSOME CHARLIE' WORKMAN (1908-UNKNOWN)

Charlie was openly admired by the top crime bosses as the most gifted killer in Murder Inc. In 1939 Charlie was tasked with killing his friend Tootsie Feinberg. Charlie obliged and when he later went to trial for the murder, Tootsie's wife, now maintained by the mob, spoke on his behalf, so garnering the legend that when Handsome Charlie kills a man, the widow stands for him in court. Charlie was eventually sentenced to life imprisonment in 1941 for the murder of Dutch Schultz. Not long after, he volunteered his services to the US Navy for a suicide mission against Japan but was refused. He was paroled in 1964 and lived out the rest of his life quietly.

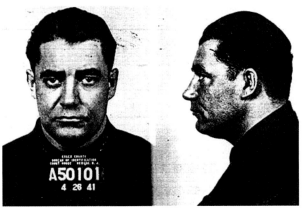

JOHN 'THE TEFLON DON' GOTTI (1940-2002, PRISON)

John Gotti rose to the head of the Gambino crime family after effecting the last known execution of a mob boss, Paul Castellano, in 1985. He earned the moniker of 'The Teflon Don' after beating a series of high-profile charges through the 1980s. No matter what the authorities threw at him, nothing stuck. He was also known in the press as 'The Dapper Don' for his style and self-promotion whereby he actively courted the press and public. Every 4th July he flouted New York's ban on fireworks with a huge display, while Andy Warhol painted his portrait for the front cover of *Time* magazine. In 1992 he finally became 'The Velcro Don' largely on account of his egotistical recklessness and the key testimony of his underboss Sammy Gravano. On being sent to jail he delivered his own obituary, 'I'll always be one of a kind. You'll never see another guy like me if you live to be 5000.' 10 years later, having died of cancer in a maximum

security state prison, thousands turned out to see his funeral procession through Queens.

IRVING 'BIG GANGY' COHEN (DATES UNKNOWN)

'Big Gangy', named for his hulking size, was one of the few members of Murder Inc. to successfully run away and disentangle himself from the mob. He quite literally ran for the trees immediately after fulfilling orders to kill his best friend Walter Sage in 1937. The mystery of Gangy's whereabouts was answered in 1939 when ex-colleagues Pretty Levine and Dukey Maffeotore went to see the film *Golden Boy* and spotted him as an extra in the film. Big Gangy had fled to Hollywood and taken up

bit-part acting under the name Jack Gordon. He would go on to appear as an extra in *It's a Wonderful Life*. Ironically, it was his portrayal of a cop on screen that got the attention of the New York authorities who hauled him back East to face trial for the murder of Sage. He was acquitted and lived out his days peacefully in Hollywood.

ARNOLD 'THE BRAIN' ROTHSTEIN (1882-1928, MURDERED)

Rothstein was the father of organised crime as we know it and the first thoroughly modern gangster. In his role as financier to the underworld he had many nicknames, 'Mr Big', 'The Man Uptown', 'The Big Bankroll', and among the younger Jewish mobsters 'Ph.G'(Pappa has gelt). Rothstein became a mentor to promising young guns such as Lucky Luciano, Meyer Lansky, Waxey Gordon and Frank Costello and by proxy fashioned the future business structure of the mob. Popular legend along with his immortalised representation as Meyer Wolfsheim in *The Great Gatsby* have cemented him as the man that fixed the 1919 World Series, though in reality it would seem he turned this proposal down. 'The Brain' was gunned down aged 46 for 'welching' on a bet he saw as fixed.

IRVING 'WAXEY GORDON' WEXLER (1888-1952, ALCATRAZ)

Wexler made his name as a pickpocket on the Lower East Side. His trick was to wax his fingers, and the name 'Waxey' stuck (Gordon was a preferred alias). It was Waxey who took the plan for large-scale bootlegging to Rothstein in 1920, and later controlled this lucrative racket across the East Coast, earning him around $2million a year. These figures didn't quite match his declared earnings of $8100 for 1930 and he was convicted for tax evasion in 1933. Once out, he tried to rebuild his empire on narcotics but was picked up in 1951 for trying to sell heroin to an undercover narcotics agent. On failing to bribe the agent he reportedly asked him to shoot him on the spot.

CHARLES 'LUCKY' LUCIANO (1897-1962)

'Lucky' was an apt nickname for Luciano, the only hood to survive being 'taken for a ride'. Caught up in The Castellammarese War, he was kidnapped by goons, beaten, stabbed and left for dead on a New York beach. But 'Lucky' wasn't dead and made sure that he emerged victorious in the war. In 1931 he became the first effective Capo di tutti Capi (boss of all bosses), presiding over a newly formed National Crime Syndicate that would represent the business interests of the Five Families of New York and other mob outfits throughout the country. This saw him listed in *Time* magazine's 100 'Builders and Titans' of the 20th Century. Luciano was sent down in 1936 for 30-50 years but after the 1942 sinking of the Normandie troop ship in New York harbour, 'Lucky' started

taking meetings in his cell with naval intelligence officers in a bid to use his muscle to guarantee the safety of the ports from enemy sabotage. He also offered invaluable contacts for espionage in Sicily and was even said to have a plan to 'whack' the Fuhrer. In 1946, in return for his wartime services, Luciano's sentence was commuted and he was exiled to Italy from where he continued to play a major part in organised crime across continents.

LLEWELYN MORRIS 'MURRAY THE CAMEL' HUMPHREYS (1899-1965)

A Chicago mobster of Welsh descent, Murray was named on account of the 'Hump' in his surname. 'The Camel' rose to become the chief political fixer and labour racketeer for the Chicago Outfit hugely respected by Capone and his successors. Murray was well connected in the political world and by his later years it was generally known that he had dined with presidents and kings across the world. 'The Camel' was also well liked among the FBI for his charm despite their constant surveillance. In bugged conversations he could often be heard to say, 'Good morning, gentlemen, and anyone listening. This is the nine o'clock meeting of the Chicago underworld.' Legend has it that on another occasion 'The Camel' having being tailed all day by FBI agents, stopped his driver and sent his car on before telling the Feds that there was no point them having two cars and that he'd ride with them.

HISTORICAL MASHUPS

PRESENTED FOR YOUR EDIFICATION AND AMUSEMENT BY THE Q.I. EMERITUS PROFESSOR OF UTTERLY SPURIOUS PSEUDO FACTS WITH A DOCTORATE IN BEFUDDLEMENT

PHILL JUPITUS

AH THERE YOU ARE! ALLOW ME TO BID YOU WELCOME TO THE **STALIN-ARCHER** INSTITUTE. IT IS HERE THAT EXPERTS IN THE FIELD OF HISTORY SPEND HOURS DISMANTLING FACTS, THEN REASSEMBLING THEM...

THESE NEWLY **FABRICATED** NUGGETS THEN FORM THE BASIS OF A BRAND NEW HISTORICAL PERSPECTIVE COMPLETELY UNENCUMBERED BY SUCH INCONVENIENCES AS **TRUTH** OR **ACCURACY**...

OUR CHALLENGE... THIS YEAR WAS TO REWRITE KEY EVENTS WITH SPECIAL ATTENTION TO THE LETTER "G"! WE HOPE YOU ENJOY OUR EFFORTS. WELL... MUST DASH AND FINISH OUR NEXT PROJECT "TONY BLAIR - MAKING CHURCHILL LOOK LIKE A PONCE"... xx

---

DRUIDS CONSTRUCT 'GONEHENGE'

PRE-HISTORY'S FIRST VANISHING PAGAN TEMPLE 'GONEHENGE' WAS DUE TO REAPPEAR SHORTLY AFTER ITS SUDDEN DISAPPEARANCE... MANY STILL WAIT...

THE RISE & FALL OF THE ROGAN EMPIRE...

needs yoghurt

WHO COULD HAVE PREDICTED THAT THE WORLD WOULD FALL UNDER THE SPELL OF A TOMATO BASED SAVOURY MEAT DISH... ITS DECLINE WAS PROMPTED BY THE POPULARITY OF THE KORMA...

THE GROGAN HORSE

Happy birthday.. Happy birthday...

ooh! I like this one!

THEY SAY THAT HELEN OF TROY'S FACE LAUNCHED A THOUSAND SHIPS... WELL THIS FORMER LEAD SINGER OF SCOTTISH INDIE SENSATIONS 'ALTERED IMAGES' LAUNCHED AT LEAST THREE 'HITS'...

ENGLISH CIVIL WAG

she seeketh shoe shoppes...

IT IS A DIFFICULT CONCEPT TO GRASP AT BEST, BUT ONCE THIS COUNTRY WAS DIVIDED BY AN OVERLY POLITE FOOTBALLER'S WIFE...

THE GREAT DIGRESSION

TY COBB? NOW THERE'S A REAL SCUMBAG!

U.S.B.C.

SHORTLY AFTER HIS ELECTION IN 1932 FRANKLIN D. ROOSEVELT STARTED AN ANECDOTE ABOUT BASEBALL. THIS ONE STORY LASTED UNTIL AMERICA ENTERED WW2 IN 1941. AND DISTRACTED MOST PEOPLE...

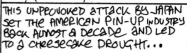

THE ATTACK ON GIRL HARBOUR

THIS UNPROVOKED ATTACK BY JAPAN SET THE AMERICAN PIN-UP INDUSTRY BACK ALMOST A DECADE AND LED TO A CHEESECAKE DROUGHT...

MAN LANDS ON MOOG

YOU MIGHT FALL RICK!

NOW WHAT

GET DOWN RICK!

KEYBOARD WIZZARD AND BON VIVEUR RICK WAKEMAN OF WEIRDO POP BAND 'YES' WAS THE "FIRST MAN ON THE MOOG" IN 1971. SADLY THIS VIOLATED THE TERMS OF THE GUARANTEE...

OSAMA BIG LADEN...

GRRRRR

He's huge

JESUS H CHRIST

HISTORY MIGHT HAVE BEEN MUCH DIFFERENT, HAD THIS 200 FOOT TALL SPIRITUAL LEADER HELD SWAY... HE WOULD HAVE BEEN EASIER TO FIND FOR A START!

THE FIRST BLOG PRESIDENCY

howdy howdy goo howdy howdy! HOWDY howdy howdy! howdy howdy! HOWDY howdy howdy! howdy howdy HOWDY! howdy howdy howdy ho

ACTUALLY THIS ONE REALLY DID HAPPEN. THE FIRST PRESIDENCY WAS BLOGGED ON 7TH NOVEMBER 2000...

29

GROWING PAINS

GRUESOME GOBBETS CONCERNING THE GHASTLY GOINGS-ON DURING PUBERTY

The DAYAK people pierce boys' penises at puberty and their grandfathers insert a PHALANG, a stud with a lump at each end, through the tip of the penis.

"GEORGE MICHAEL" is cockney rhyming slang for "MENSTRUAL CYCLE"

← OESTROGEN

menstrual cycle

TRADITIONALLY Malay boys were circumsized when they reached puberty, rather than at birth. Ouch....

PUBERTAL SPURT — contrary to what you might fear, the term actually describes the sudden surge in a boy's growth rate during his teenage years.

← TESTOSTERONE

SEX

THE WORD VIRGIN ORIGINALLY REFERRED TO A GIRL WHO HAD NEVER HAD SEX. GERMAN & FRENCH BOTH HAVE A WORD FOR A MALE VIRGIN — "JÜNGLING" IN GERMAN — "PUCEAU" IN FRENCH — BUT ENGLISH DOESN'T.

The first BRA was patented as the "backless brassiere" (from the French word for 'upper arm') in 1914, by New York socialite Mary Phelps Jacob

BREASTS COME IN ALL DIFFERENT SHAPES & SIZES

Cherry Denman's GUIDE to the LITERARY BOSOM

THE JANE AUSTEN

THE MARTIN AMIS

THE VIRGINIA WOOLF

THE HENRY FIELDING

THE MAYA ANGELOU

A BOY'S VOICE

breaks during puberty because his vocal cords get about 60% longer.

UP UNTIL THAT POINT, GIRL'S AND BOY'S VOCAL CORDS ARE THE SAME LENGTH.

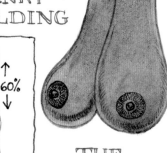

↑ 60% ↓

According to Captain Cook, Tahitians had their buttocks tattooed black after puberty.

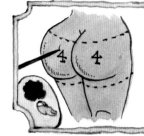

PUBARCHE

The first appearance of pubic hair

There is an old Slavic custom of mothers slapping their daughters when they have their first period.

FROM THE MID-1500s TO THE LATE 1800s, BOYS WERE DRESS-ED IN GOWNS OR DRESSES UNTIL THE AGE OF FIVE TO SEVEN, WHEN THEY WERE 'BREECHED' OR PUT IN THEIR FIRST PAIR OF TROUSERS.

EVEN RAMESES II SUFFERED FROM ACNE

·——·

PUBESCENT = covered with soft, downy hair.

Five Go Gallivanting After Ghosts!

JULIAN would like to be an actuary or an exotic dancer.

GEORGINA likes to be called 'George' and is a bit of a tomboy.

ANNE likes the sort of things girls like, but not girls like George.

DICK: Likes cake – that's basically it.

...and not forgetting Timmy the Dog!!

Photography by Jim Marks

Julian, Dick, Anne, George and Timmy have heard rumours that the Olde Manor House is haunted. Knowing about the Amityville[1] and Borely Rectory[2] hoaxes they have decided to investigate...

"Come on", says Julian, "Let's gain entry through this window. As it's open we won't need a gablock[3] and surprisingly, as we have no intention of stealing, we are not committing a crime, although we are trespassing - which is a tort[4]."

But what's this? They're not alone.

"I thought you said this place was empty?", gowls[5] Dick.

"Gosh! Even a perfect vacuum is not technically 'empty'", opines Julian, "Not at the Planck scale[6]".

"Hello Children", says Miss Elizabethe, the gothic[7] housekeeper. "Feel free to look round but I warn you, this place is haunted. If someone doesn't exorcise the ghost soon then the market value of this property will sink even further, just as the *Daily Mail* predicted".

Julian is suspicious.

"Hmmmm. According to the *QI Book of Supernatural Arse-Gravy* Miss Elizabethe's 'My Chemical Romance' T-shirt is more emo than goth. I wonder..."

But just then...

Wooooahhh!

Anne has heard a disembodied voice. "Perhaps it's a restless spirit trying to contact us from beyond the grave? After all the Chamba people of the Cameroon/Nigerian border hold that the incomprehensible babbling of infants and the old is the language of ghosts."

"Don't worry Anne", laughs Dick. "According to the book the voices are probably in your head and could be symptoms of psychosis or perhaps just cake deprivation."

"And you're not alone Anne", adds Julian. "You might be hearing things but Dick is seeing them. Look, the sunlight projecting through the window is creating an illusion similar to Pepper's Ghost[8] developed by Henry Dircks and John Henry Pepper and first demonstrated theatrically during a scene in Charles Dickens' *The Haunted Man* in 1863."

The gang have found a trail of non-newtonian[9] goo?

"Could it be ectoplasm?" asks Anne.

"Do you mean 'ectoplasm' in the strict biological sense of the word, that is 'the outer layer of cytoplasm of a cell'." asks George.

"I think I'll just listen to the voices in my head," reflects Anne.

"No Timmy – Don't eat it. Ectoplasm (in the spiritual sense) is supposedly dangerous to touch."

"Bollocks", retorts Timmy. "Ectoplasm is also supposedly destroyed by light and smells of gorgonzola cheese. This smells like the type of hygroscopic mucus shed during slug copulation."

"Blimey", says Dick, "Timmy can talk."

Timmy has found a tarot deck and pulled out 'death'.

"Bad luck Timmy", says George. "Using tarot for divination began in 1781 with Antoine Court de Gébelin's publication of *'Le Monde Primitif'*[10] which suggests the symbolism of Tarot cards represent a survival of arcane knowledge into the modern world. As such you're probably about to die."

Dick, Anne and George try guessing the future with the cards.

"Tarot, or Tarocchi to give them their original name, are just a different style of playing card popular from the mid-fifteenth century." counters Julian. "You're just as likely to be able to predict your future playing Happy Families or Snap."

" I don't think too many happy families have lived here" chortles Dick, "Look, a warning written in blood, the same medium used by the German Dr Faustus for making his pact with Mephistopheles[11]."

Look out Dick!

"Look what you've done Julian", groans George, "you've scorned the tarot and now we're all doomed. If only you weren't so cynical."

"Of course I'm not a true cynic in the Greek sense," rejoinders Julian, "although I do believe that the road to virtue is to free oneself from any influence such as wealth, fame, or power, which have no value in Nature."

"And anyway", he adds, "Look, it's not a ghostly warning but simply a useful health and safety message about the unevenness of the steps written in the heraldic tincture 'gules' or 'red' as we call it - the colour internationally recognised as suggesting danger.

Get up Dick, Dick..."

Dick is finally revived by the smell of cake.

"Smells like Génoise cake, an Italian sponge cake which gains its volume from air suspended in the batter during mixing rather than a leavening agent." notes Dick.

Dick's greed carries him and the gang down a dark corridor, deep into the bowels of the house.

"It is a cake," shrieks Dick, "But more like 'Gob', a type of chocolate cake associated with the Pennsylvanian Amish." Dick knows a lot about cake.

But just as the gang are about to make a grab for the gateau...

"IT'S THE GHOST!"
"It's a Ghoul, perhaps, as some cognitive neuroscientists now think, caused by the stimulation of the temporal lobes brought on by changes in the earth's geomagnetic field," cries Anne.

"No it's not", declaims the insufferably smug Julian. "It's Elizabethe, the emo housekeeper, hoping that reports of ghosts combined with the global recession would suppress the value of the house enough for her to buy it herself."

"But that's obtaining pecuniary advantage by deception," exclaims George, "an offence under the Theft Act of 1968. She's going to Gaol."

"As the American writer Lloyd Douglas once said," drones Julian, "If a man harbors any sort of fear, it makes him landlord to a ghost."

"Can anyone else hear a voice saying 'Kill Julian'" asks Anne.

FOOTNOTES 1: Amityville is in Suffolk County, New York, and features in the novel *The Amityville Horror*, based on a real-life multiple murder case and the subsequent alleged haunting of the crime scene at 112 Ocean Avenue. 2: Borley Rectory A Victorian mansion in the village of Borley, Essex, built in 1863. After unexplained 'events' in the late 1920s paranormal investigator and confidence trickster Harry Price claimed the site as 'The Most Haunted House in England'. It was destroyed by fire in 1939. 3: Gablock A dialect word for an iron crowbar, c.1746. 4: Tort In English Law, the breach of a duty imposed by law, whereby some person acquires a right of action for damages. 5: Gowl To howl, yell, cry or whine (14th century). 6: Planck Scale The Planck length is around 1.616 x 10⁻³⁵ metres. When describing time or gravity at this scale, normal physics stops working and the mysterious rules of quantum physics take over. 7: Gothic A genre of fiction characterised by suspenseful plots involving supernatural or macabre elements as in Horace Walpole's 1765 *The Castle of Otranto* which is subtitled 'a Gothic story'. 8: Pepper's Ghost An illusion used in magic tricks, using a plate glass and special lighting to make objects seem to appear or disappear. 9: A non-Newtonian fluid is one whose molecules do not obey Isaac Newton's rules of motion e.g. quicksand and custard, both of which get thicker the more you mix them. 10: Antoine Court de Gébelin (ca.1719-84) was a former Protestant pastor who initiated the interpretation of the Tarot as an arcane repository of hermetic knowledge (as opposed to being simply a set of playing cards) in an essay included in his *Le Monde primitif*, vol viii, 1781. 11: Christopher Marlowe's *Dr Faustus* sells his soul to the devil in return for power and knowledge.

Gee-Kwiz!

With one person as quizmaster, you can play this at home. Five rounds of 8 questions each; 2 points for a correct answer, but playing your joker before any one round doubles your score on that round.

Let's warm up with an easy one...

GEOGRAPHY!

1. What do they do at Lloyds of London when a ship is reported sunk anywhere in the world?
2. What do most Spaniards have after lunch?
3. Name a famous brand name of a German wine drunk in Germany.
4. Whose national flag is this?
5. What's the only part of mainland South America that is not an independent country?
6. Which country in the world is home to the ethnic groups the Bangi, the Binga, the Benga and the Banga?
7. What's quite interesting about the tides in the Mediterranean?
8. Which English county is Wigan in?

> A survey by Heinz in 2008 found that many British children don't like vegetables at all, with aubergines being the most hated. Amongst other things the survey discovered was that rather than eat vegetables, an astonishing seven out of 10 British children hide them around the house.

GARDENING!

1. Where do Welsh onions come from?
2. What do the American gooseberry, the Tahiti gooseberry, the Cape gooseberry, the Coromandel gooseberry, the Barbados gooseberry and the Chinese gooseberry have in common?
3. Which vegetable has the same number of chromosomes as a gorilla?
4. Where is the greatest and densest diversity of plant life on the planet to be found in a single place?
5. Approximately how many celery seeds weigh 1oz (28g)?
6. How many parsnips have won the Nobel Prize for Literature?
7. What did John Boyd Dunlop find in his garden that enabled him to become world famous?
8. What kind of fruit would you find in a plum pudding?

> QI's favourite G-Man is the great American columnist and sports writer Lewis Grizzard, who is an absolute mine of laconic pith. This for instance: 'I don't think I'll get married again. I think I'll just find a woman I don't like and give her a house.' Here are some other G-related Men.

G-MEN!

1. He had a biscuit named after him, and was born in a town after which a different biscuit is named. Name the biscuits.
2. What G connects all these men? Burhan Asaf Belge, Conrad Hilton, George Sanders, Herbert Hutner, Joshua S. Cosden, Jack Ryan, Michael O'Hara, Felipe de Alba, Frédéric Prinz von Anhalt and the inventor of the hologram?
3. Of which eponymous Oscar winner was it said 'he was everything the voting members of the Academy would like to have been - moral, tan and thin'?
4. How did the great Spanish pianist and composer Granados die?

5. Who famously described Ingrid Bergman as a 'nice woman who speaks five languages but can't act in any of them'?
6. Whom did Colonel Gaddafi claim wrote the Works of Shakespeare?
7. Which G-man was born in the same year as William Shakespeare, the year that Michelangelo died?
   This next one is seriously difficult: bonus points for anyone who gets it right.
8. According to James Joyce, the three greatest literary talents of the 19th century were Leo Tolstoy, Rudyard Kipling and ....
   (fill in the blank)

GREATNESS!

1. What was the first wife of Herod the Great called?
2. What familiar modern technology is named after King Canute the Great's grandfather?
3. What was the first building in the world to be taller than the Great Pyramid of Cheops at Giza?
4. What was the name of the father of the first and greatest Duke of Marlborough?
5. Who was Sophie Auguste Friederike von Anhalt-Zerbst?
6. What is the name of the storm twice as big as the earth that has been raging for 300 years?
7. The cathedral treasury at Aachen has a famous collection of sacred relics, among which are the tights of Jesus' father, St Joseph. Four of these sacred relics are known as *The Great Relics*. Two points for each one of them you can name.
8. George Graham (c.1674-1751) was the greatest instrument-maker of his age, the Master of the Clockmakers' Company and a Fellow of the Royal Society. He is buried in Westminster Abbey. He invented something that he might easily have called a Boyle, but he didn't. What did he call it?

> Baltasar Gracián y Morales (1601-1658) was a Spanish Jesuit and philosopher who influenced La Rochefoucauld, Voltaire, Nietzsche and, especially, Schopenhauer (who considered his Criticón one of the best books ever written). In The Art of Worldly Wisdom (1647), Gracián wrote: 'The greatest wisdom often consists in ignorance'. So, feel free to feel smug if you get all of these wrong.

GENERAL IGNORANCE!

1. How many possible pronunciations of the letter 'G' are there in English?
2. What is the largest moon in the Solar System?
3. How many galaxies are visible to the naked eye?
4. Who was President of the Olympic Games in 12 AD?
5. What contains enough steel to make 64 double decker buses or 16 Chieftain tanks but only costs £3.60 every time it is used?
6. What word beginning with 'G' was invented by the Dutch chemist van Helmont in about 1600 and is said to be the single most successful invention of a word whose author is actually known?
7. Penultimately, a question on G-forces. What travels well over twice as fast as the fastest jet fighter with its afterburners on, and almost twice as fast as the space shuttle on re-entry?
8. What is Spurius Carvilius Ruga's claim to fame?

Answers on p94

G

IN THE GARDEN

GODWOTTERY~
Affected, archaic, or excessively elaborate speech or writing concerning gardens.
From T.E.Brown's poem "A GARDEN IS A LOVESOME THING, GOD WOT."

GNOME~ a dwarfish creature.
~ a maxim or aphorism.

GRAMINACEOUS ~ Grassy

GLEY ~ a sticky waterlogged soil.

GNOMON the rod or pin on a sundial that shows the time by the position of its shadow.

GOWK ···· a cuckoo

GINKO AN ornamental tree

GALLIMAUFRY a jumble or medley

GINGLMUS a hingelike joint ~a knee~

GERMINATION putting forth shoots

GUM BOOTS

GOWAN a daisy

37

HOW TO SEE GULLS

1. People are often surprised to see seagulls far inland.

'They're sea gulls!' they cry. 'They should be by the sea!' But there's something even more surprising about this: *seagulls don't exist.* Like the Cabbage White Butterfly, the Seagull is a name unknown to science. Ornithologists insist on the word 'gull', several varieties of which spend their whole lives miles from the sea.

2. You won't see gulls at Sellafield.

They're in the fridge. Any bird that lands at the accident-prone Cumbrian nuclear power plant – which a lot of gulls do – gets shot by snipers, to prevent it carrying radioactive contamination to neighbouring areas. The ever-growing mountain of avian corpses is classed both as 'low-level nuclear waste' and as 'putrescent waste', and therefore can't be tipped on a dump.

3. Keep your mouth shut where gulls are concerned.

Many local authorities in Britain spend fortunes on gull control, fearing that the birds can infect tourists with salmonella through their droppings. Experts pooh-pooh this. A leading gullologist writes: 'Only 2.7% of gulls are infected. For a human to get salmonella, he would have to walk around looking upwards with his mouth open. A rare infected bird would then have to defecate straight into his mouth and he would have to swallow it.'

4. And whose little chick are you, then, hmm?

In some gull species, parents don't recognise their own chicks until 5 - 7 days after hatching. Before the chicks are mobile, there's no need to know what they look like — only to remember where they are. Orphaned chicks often stowaway in a neighbouring nest. The evolutionary risk of the parents not feeding one of their own outweighs the cost of feeding an interloper — on the other hand, if they do happen to spot the intruder, they kill the scrounging little bastard.

5. The Seagull Diet.

Gull eggs can fetch four quid each in the restaurants of posh London clubs. And prices are rising, due to a disastrous decline in gull numbers over recent years. Nobody knows why the gulls are disappearing. It couldn't possibly be because fat toffs have scoffed all their eggs, could it?

6. Can you see what it is yet?

When birds cause aircraft to crash, investigators analyse the bits of beak, blood, guts and feathers adhering to the wreckage, to establish the particular species of bird involved (often gulls or geese). To gather this gunk, which scientists call 'snarge', they spray the piece of plane with water, and then wipe it down with paper towels, which are sent to the Feather Identification Lab in Washington, DC.

7. Big-eyed gulls.

"HAVEN'T SLEPT FOR WEE THREEKS"

The swallow-tailed gull of the Galapagos Islands is the only fully nocturnal seabird on earth. It has enormous eyes, the better to hunt squid as they rise to the surface of the sea at night in search of plankton.

8. The Seagull Effect.

FLAP FLAP

In 1963, the Father of Chaos Theory, Edward Lorenz (1917-2008), explained how tiny events can have large and unpredictable effects elsewhere. His example: the flap of a seagull's wings affecting the weather many miles away. Years later, he was due to present a paper at a conference, but hadn't come up with a title. It was sent to press using the heading *Predictability: Does the flap of a butterfly's wings in Brazil set off a tornado in Texas?* Boo! Join The QI Campaign to Reassert the Centrality of Gulls to Chaos Theory!

9. Gulls don't just eat chips and ice cream, you know!

Off the coast of Argentina, Kelp Gulls have taken to lunching on Southern Right Whales. They simply land on their backs and start eating them alive, pecking away at their skin and blubber. The whales are in real danger, not just from their huge wounds, but because they spend so much time evading gull attacks, disastrously disrupting their sleep cycles.

10. And now see what gulls have done!

They've only gone and led to yet ANOTHER new science! Ethology, the study of animal behaviour, was pioneered by Niko Tinbergen (1907-88). His understanding of 'pre-programming' – animals knowing how to behave as soon as they're born – came from studying the feeding

behaviour of herring gulls. When a chick pecks at the red spot on the adult's beak, the parent sicks up a gorgeous load of fish paste into the baby's gullet. Tinbergen found it's the spot, not the parent, that counts: chicks respond the same to a lump of wood with a red blob painted on it.

I must down to the seas again to the vagrant gypsy life,
To the gull's way and the whale's way where the wind's like a whetted knife.

JOHN MASEFIELD (1878-1967) 'Sea-Fever'

am I great?

'He's great'... 'That was great'... 'I had a great time.' Everything these days seems to be great. It's a word we use every day – but what does it mean to really be Great? Are you personally Great or just 'OK'? *Why not take our fun coffee-break quiz to find out...*

Q1: It's Friday afternoon, you've had a really hard week and you just want to go home and curl up with a book but your friends want you to go to the pub. **Do you:**

A: Tell them you're just not up to it and take a rain check for next week?
B: Agree to go along 'just for one'?
C: Single-handedly take on the might of the Persian Empire?

Q2: Your boss calls you in and tells you he's had a great team-building idea – a karaoke night for the whole office – and he wants you to arrange it. **Do you:**

A: Ask the girls in the office if they know a good karaoke pub you could go to – even if it's a disaster at least you can all have a drink?
B: Get on the phone to admin and demand they buy a karaoke machine – on expenses?
C: Develop a novel system of notation for devotional chant melodies inspired directly by the whisperings of the Holy Spirit?

Q3: You're halfway through a romantic dinner à deux with that dreamy guy from sales when, biting into a crusty roll – crunch! – you break a tooth. **Do you:**

A: Excuse yourself for a moment, rush to the loo and take a handful of aspirin for the pain – this chance may never come again and the dentist can wait for the morning?
B: Pretend you've had a call on your mobile summoning you home straight away, but not before you reschedule the date!
C: Take an extended tour of Europe to learn the modern science of dentistry, returning home in triumph to your backward nation to dazzle the peasantry with your newfound skills?

Q4: It's not easy dating when you've got young kids – it can scare the men off. So, you're having lunch with the new man in your life and he asks the fateful question: 'Have you got any kids?' **What do you say?**

A: Lie and say no. If the relationship goes any further AND he's really the one for you then he won't mind.
B: Ask if it would make any difference to him before answering.
C: Proudly boast of your 56 sons and 44 daughters.

Q5: You've hit a rough patch with your man – he just wants to watch football and play on the Xbox, neither of which activities were in your marriage vows as far as you can remember. Perhaps you can rekindle the flame – but how? **Do you:**

A: Take a bath and slip into that little black dress that used to drive him wild, before offering him a game that's not available on any Xbox!?
B: Make the best of a bad deal. After all, isn't this how all men end up? Perhaps it's time to get a hobby… or a lover!
C: Arrange for his immediate removal by Imperial troops to a distant palace where your lover's brother can quietly strangle him?

Q6: You really need a loan but you're worried that your menial job title might look bad on the application form. **What do you put down?**

A: 'Secretary' – it's the truth and the bank will appreciate your honesty.
B: 'Executive Assistant' – it makes you sound like management and isn't a complete lie.
C: 'King of the world, great king, mighty king, King of Babylon, King of the land of Sumer and Akkad, King of the four quarters, son of Cambyses, King of Anshan, grandson of Cyrus, descendant of Teispes, progeny of an unending royal line, whose rule Bel and Nabu cherish, whose kingship they desire for their hearts' pleasures.'

Q7: The boss has requested you attend a posh reception for potential graduates. The booze is flowing freely BUT you've been explicitly told to set a good example and not get drunk. The waiter comes up and asks what you want to drink. **What do you say?**

A: Ask him to get you an orange juice with a double vodka in it – who's to know?
B: Take one glass of champagne and make it last – you want to look relaxed but you're keen to stay focused.
C: Tell the waiter that you only drink pure water from the river Ganga, for it is the Water of Immortality.

Q8: You're at a dinner party and a guy keeps going on about how much he does for charity. He then rudely asks you what you've done. **What's your response?**

A: Mumble something about always buying the Big Issue.
B: Tell him that you don't like to talk about your charity work – it's vulgar.
C: Crisply draw to his attention the 84,000 Buddhist monuments, shrines, temples and monastic residences you have built across Asia.

Q9: It's Halloween and you and some mates have stayed up drinking. The conversation has moved onto the spooky subject of what sort of funeral you'd all like. **So how do you want to go out?**

A: Just a simple cremation thanks. Forget the flowers and give the money to charity.
B: A big party. No crying. Just lots of music and lots of drink. I want you to celebrate my life.
C: Return my body to the Steppe. Should my cortege meet anyone or anything en route they must be instantly killed so that none know where I lie. When you bury me, divert a river over my grave so that I may enjoy eternal peace.

Q10: Your kingdom is being repeatedly over-run by marauding Vikings but no matter how much you pay them they just keep coming back for more. **Do you:**

A: Decide to call in sick and snuggle up in front of daytime TV with a cup of tea and a big box of chocolates?
B: Buy the Viking chief a Bacardi Breezer and suggest he makes contact with his 'inner woman'?
C: Completely re-arrange the administration and military organisation of your country to respond to multiple threats over extended time periods. Combine this with a radical overhaul of the educational system, a rewriting of the laws of the country and a unique defensive building programme which you hope will, in time, neutralise the threat.

So how did you do?

Mostly A:

Frankly you're more grating than great. It's time to take charge of your life and stop just saying what you think other people want to hear. Did Hitler bother about what people said about him? No – and neither should you.

Mostly B:

You might be great company but you're not 'Great' in the strictly historical sense that is meant here. Being a supreme being is rarely about having a laugh with your mates, it's about paranoid delusions, megalomania and Messianic self-belief. You need to work on these.

Mostly C:

You're Great!

You have the ambition of ALEXANDER THE GREAT (Q1); the dedication of ST GREGORY THE GREAT (Q2); the work ethic of TSAR PETER THE GREAT (Q3); the fruitful loins of RAMESES THE GREAT (Q4); the man-management flair of CATHERINE THE GREAT (Q5); the PR skills of CYRUS THE GREAT (Q6); the great taste of AKBAR THE GREAT (Q7); the generosity of ASHOKA THE GREAT (Q8); the forward-planning smarts of GHENGIS (THE GREAT) KHAN (Q9); and the legislative and supervisory can-do of ALFRED THE GREAT (Q10).

But you're probably short on friends.

QUITE INTERESTING
GOLF

The world's most challenging 9-hole golf course – designed by the QI Elves using real locations from all over the world ...and beyond.

HOLE 1: LOST CITY COURSE, SOUTH AFRICA
The first hole at the QI golf course also doubles as the par-3 thirteenth hole at the Lost City Course in the Pilanesberg Game Reserve, South Africa. The green, which is shaped like the continent of Africa, is protected by 9 bunkers and a crocodile pit that one must play directly over.

HOLE 2: LEGEND GOLF, SOUTH AFRICA
The second hole is only 50 miles or so south of hole one, and can be found at the Legend Golf and Safari Resort. This course's 19th hole is known as the million-dollar par 3. The tee is perched over 1,300 ft (396 m) up, at the top of Hanglip Mountain – access only by helicopter – with the putting green at the bottom of the vertical drop. A hole-in-one here and you will receive $1,000,000.

HOLE 3: MOUNT MERAPI, INDONESIA
Keep your eyes on your caddie at the Mount Merapi golf course in Indonesia. If he runs, it's probably best to follow suit as this is the closest golf course to an active volcano in the world. The 18th hole is just outside Merapi's mandatory evacuation zone and the course closes whenever there is an eruption; the last one was in 2006.

HOLE 4: THE ARIKIKAPAKAPA COURSE, NEW ZEALAND
Also troubled by volcanic activity is The Arikikapakapa Course on New Zealand's North Island. The course has a number of unusual hazards including bubbling mud pools, steam vents and strange sulphur mounds. Best to aim to the right of the 14th green as the left is guarded by a monster of a thermal crater.

HOLE 5: URBAN GOLF, HAMBURG

Urban Golf, that is golf played in a city centre rather than on a golf course, was the invention of German Torsten Schilling, a former TV set-designer who found himself playing in hotel corridors to pass the time. The game is played with a leather ball stuffed with goose feathers in order to prevent damage and is usually only played with two clubs so that proponents can quickly scarper if the police should take offence. Usually a bin is designated as the hole, while lamp-posts are trees and drains are bunkers.

HOLE 6: UUMMANNAQ, GREENLAND

In the 1890s, living in Vermont, Rudyard Kipling invented 'snow golf' a game involving red balls and tin cans for holes. His spirit is still alive with the World Ice Golf Championship that takes place at Santa Claus's home course of Uummannaq every New Year. Polar bears are not an inconsiderable hazard, and your card will warn of the risks of falling down seal breathing holes.

HOLE 7: CAMP BONIFAS, KOREA

Natural hazards are not the problem at the Republic of Korea's Army post, Camp Bonifas. It has a 'golf course' which consists of a single par-3 hole with an astroturf green that is surrounded on three sides by minefields. It is not unknown for a wayward drive to land out-of-bounds and set off one of the explosives.

HOLE 8: CLUB DE GOLF RIO LLUTA, CHILE

Club de Golf Rio Lluta is the driest golf course in the world as its position would suggest, in the Atacama desert, the driest desert in the world. Rain never stops play here, in fact, it has never rained in the history of the club, so there is not a single blade of grass anywhere to be seen. Make sure you hit the fairways that are marked with chalk lines and you might find the putting green which is created with oil and dirt.

HOLE 9: OUTER SPACE

Alan Shepard was the first man to hit a golf ball on the Moon, hitting a shot in 1971 that he claimed went 'miles and miles and miles'. It was later estimated that his shots had travelled only 200 to 300 yards. A more difficult hole is the elves' 9th hole which begins at the international space station; in 2006, Russian cosmonaut Mikhail Tyurin hit a shot from there which will have carried around a million miles, but will never have hit any green as the ball would have burned up in the atmosphere before reaching earth.

44

GROG,
GIN, GAS, GREEN PARK,
&
A GLOBE-TROTTING GOAT

by way of Pickled Cabbage, a Pickled Ear & the Portobello Road

SEAFARING AND BINGE DRINKING HAVE ALWAYS BEEN ESSENTIAL ELEMENTS OF
THE BRITISH CHARACTER, AND THEY HAVE HELPED TO SHAPE THE NATION'S
HISTORY IN SOME REMARKABLE AND UNEXPECTED WAYS

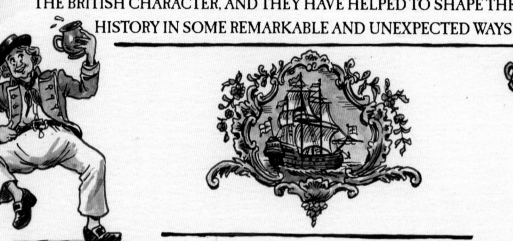

The naval drink known as GROG was named after Admiral Edward Vernon (1684–1757), whose nickname 'Old Grog', came from the grogram cloak he always wore. (Grogram, from the French *gros grain*, was a coarse cloth made of silk, mohair and wool, sometimes stiffened with gum.) Vernon was concerned about the effects of serving neat rum to ships' crews. So, at Port Royal, in August 1740, he issued an order from HMS *Burford*, to tackle the 'pernicious custom of the seamen drinking their allowance of rum in drams, and often at once, which is attended by many fatal effects to their morale as well as to their health.' Henceforth, their daily ration of half a pint of rum was to be mixed with a quart of water. The practice, soon adopted by the rest of the Fleet, lasted for over two centuries and, although by the end it had evaporated to just an eighth of a pint of rum (59 ml) diluted with a quarter of a pint (118 ml) of water, the Royal Navy only finally discontinued it in 1970.

Vernon was a remarkable man. The son of one of William III's Secretaries of State, he managed to find time to serve as an MP as well as a seaman and, in 1745, he was to prevent French reinforcements reaching Bonnie Prince Charlie's Jacobite rebels. He had earlier fought against the Spanish, and in November 1739 captured their colony Porto Bello (now in Panama) 'with six ships only'. This victory was hugely popular back in Blighty. In 1740, the same year he invented grog, Vernon received the Freedom of the City of London. The Portobello Road (as well as an area of Dublin and another in Edinburgh) was named after the battle; the song *Rule Britannia* was composed as part of the victory celebrations; and George Washington's older brother Lawrence, who had served under Vernon in the Caribbean as a Captain of Marines, returned home to Virginia and renamed the family plantation 'Mount Vernon' in his commander's honour. *

The engagement at Porto Bello was part of the curiously named 'War of Jenkins's Ear'. In 1731, a Captain Robert Jenkins was transporting sugar from Jamaica to London in the ship *Rebecca* when he was stopped and boarded by the Spanish coast guard, who accused him of carrying contraband. To discover where he had stowed the treasure, they tied Jenkins's wrists and ran him up the rigging, yanking him around to get him to talk. Jenkins kept his mouth shut, so the Captain of the coastguard hacked off his ear with a sword and advised him to take it back to King George. Seven years later, Jenkins attended a parliamentary committee investigating disputes with Spain and took along what he claimed was his ear, which he had pickled in a jar of rum. The bottled ear was waved about and the mob bayed for revenge, forcing the PM, Robert Walpole, to declare war on Spain and its ally France.

*Four Royal Navy warships have also been named after Admiral Vernon, as well as the shorebase HMS *Vernon* in Portsmouth, which was operative from 1923 to 1986. Home of the Navy's Torpedo and Anti-Submarine Branch (TAS) and Diving School, for several years in the 1960s it was commanded by Captain H.L. 'Harpy' Lloyd CBE, DSC RN, father of John Lloyd, the editor of this Annual.

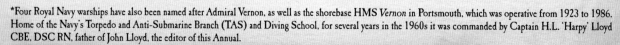

by ADRIAN TEAL, Efq; MMIX

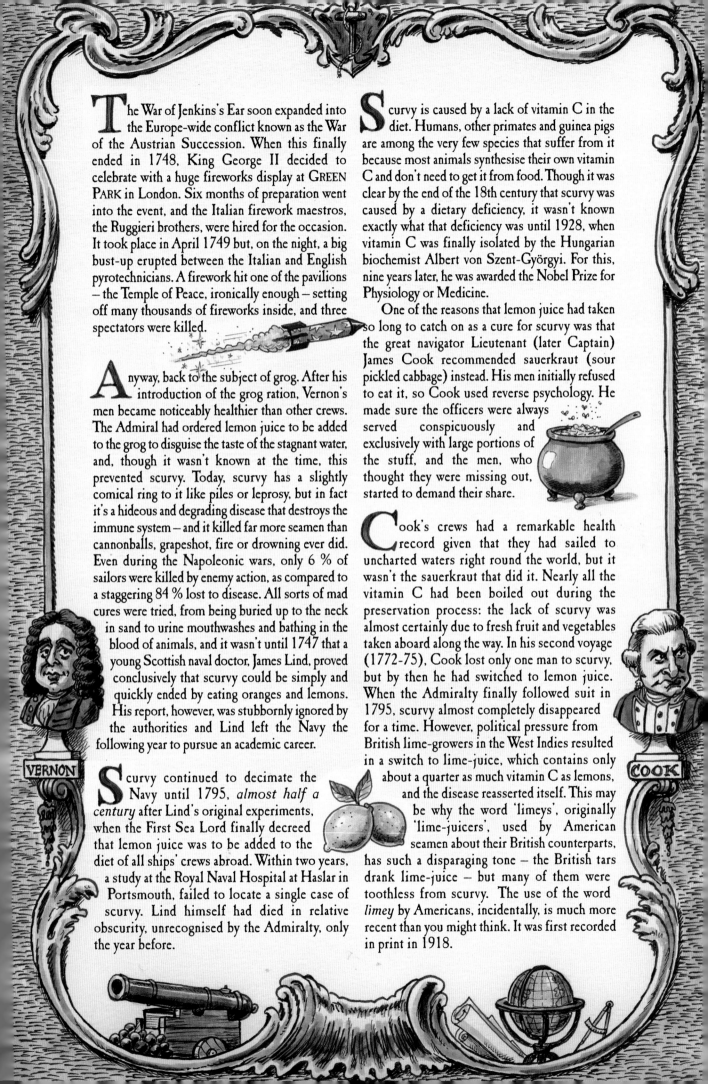

The War of Jenkins's Ear soon expanded into the Europe-wide conflict known as the War of the Austrian Succession. When this finally ended in 1748, King George II decided to celebrate with a huge fireworks display at GREEN PARK in London. Six months of preparation went into the event, and the Italian firework maestros, the Ruggieri brothers, were hired for the occasion. It took place in April 1749 but, on the night, a big bust-up erupted between the Italian and English pyrotechnicians. A firework hit one of the pavilions – the Temple of Peace, ironically enough – setting off many thousands of fireworks inside, and three spectators were killed.

Anyway, back to the subject of grog. After his introduction of the grog ration, Vernon's men became noticeably healthier than other crews. The Admiral had ordered lemon juice to be added to the grog to disguise the taste of the stagnant water, and, though it wasn't known at the time, this prevented scurvy. Today, scurvy has a slightly comical ring to it like piles or leprosy, but in fact it's a hideous and degrading disease that destroys the immune system – and it killed far more seamen than cannonballs, grapeshot, fire or drowning ever did. Even during the Napoleonic wars, only 6 % of sailors were killed by enemy action, as compared to a staggering 84 % lost to disease. All sorts of mad cures were tried, from being buried up to the neck in sand to urine mouthwashes and bathing in the blood of animals, and it wasn't until 1747 that a young Scottish naval doctor, James Lind, proved conclusively that scurvy could be simply and quickly ended by eating oranges and lemons. His report, however, was stubbornly ignored by the authorities and Lind left the Navy the following year to pursue an academic career.

VERNON

Scurvy continued to decimate the Navy until 1795, *almost half a century* after Lind's original experiments, when the First Sea Lord finally decreed that lemon juice was to be added to the diet of all ships' crews abroad. Within two years, a study at the Royal Naval Hospital at Haslar in Portsmouth, failed to locate a single case of scurvy. Lind himself had died in relative obscurity, unrecognised by the Admiralty, only the year before.

Scurvy is caused by a lack of vitamin C in the diet. Humans, other primates and guinea pigs are among the very few species that suffer from it because most animals synthesise their own vitamin C and don't need to get it from food. Though it was clear by the end of the 18th century that scurvy was caused by a dietary deficiency, it wasn't known exactly what that deficiency was until 1928, when vitamin C was finally isolated by the Hungarian biochemist Albert von Szent-Györgyi. For this, nine years later, he was awarded the Nobel Prize for Physiology or Medicine.

One of the reasons that lemon juice had taken so long to catch on as a cure for scurvy was that the great navigator Lieutenant (later Captain) James Cook recommended sauerkraut (sour pickled cabbage) instead. His men initially refused to eat it, so Cook used reverse psychology. He made sure the officers were always served conspicuously and exclusively with large portions of the stuff, and the men, who thought they were missing out, started to demand their share.

Cook's crews had a remarkable health record given that they had sailed to uncharted waters right round the world, but it wasn't the sauerkraut that did it. Nearly all the vitamin C had been boiled out during the preservation process: the lack of scurvy was almost certainly due to fresh fruit and vegetables taken aboard along the way. In his second voyage (1772-75), Cook lost only one man to scurvy, but by then he had switched to lemon juice. When the Admiralty finally followed suit in 1795, scurvy almost completely disappeared for a time. However, political pressure from British lime-growers in the West Indies resulted in a switch to lime-juice, which contains only about a quarter as much vitamin C as lemons, and the disease reasserted itself. This may be why the word 'limeys', originally 'lime-juicers', used by American seamen about their British counterparts, has such a disparaging tone – the British tars drank lime-juice – but many of them were toothless from scurvy. The use of the word *limey* by Americans, incidentally, is much more recent than you might think. It was first recorded in print in 1918.

COOK

GROG, GIN, GAS, GREEN PARK...

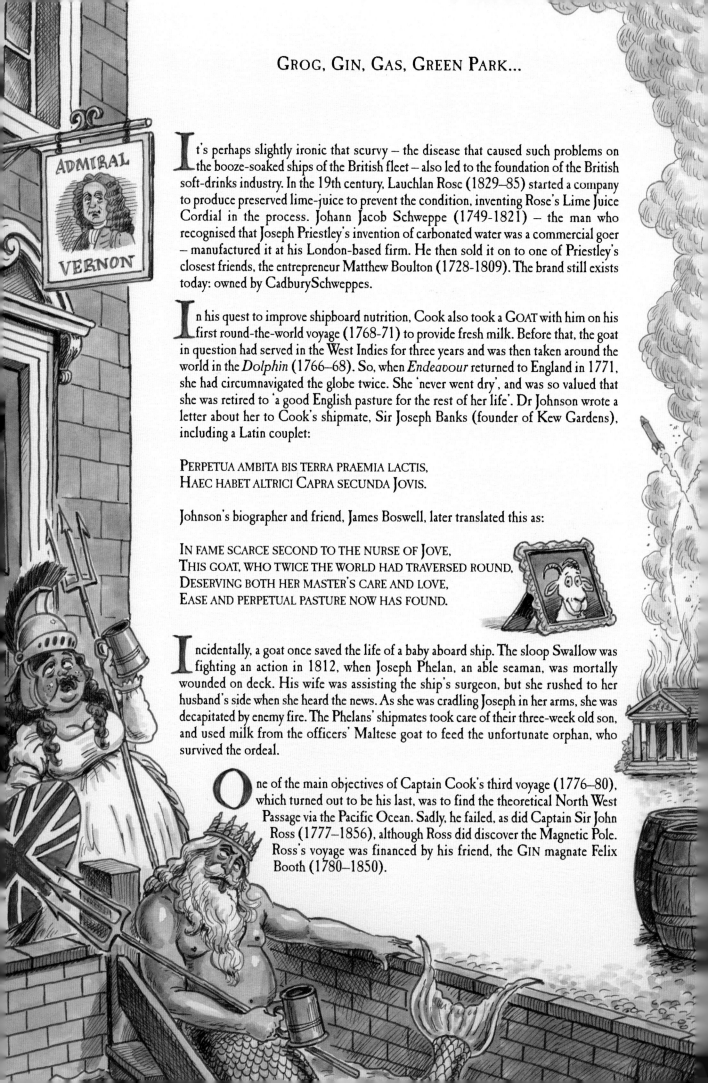

It's perhaps slightly ironic that scurvy – the disease that caused such problems on the booze-soaked ships of the British fleet – also led to the foundation of the British soft-drinks industry. In the 19th century, Lauchlan Rose (1829–85) started a company to produce preserved lime-juice to prevent the condition, inventing Rose's Lime Juice Cordial in the process. Johann Jacob Schweppe (1749-1821) – the man who recognised that Joseph Priestley's invention of carbonated water was a commercial goer – manufactured it at his London-based firm. He then sold it on to one of Priestley's closest friends, the entrepreneur Matthew Boulton (1728-1809). The brand still exists today: owned by CadburySchweppes.

In his quest to improve shipboard nutrition, Cook also took a GOAT with him on his first round-the-world voyage (1768-71) to provide fresh milk. Before that, the goat in question had served in the West Indies for three years and was then taken around the world in the *Dolphin* (1766–68). So, when *Endeavour* returned to England in 1771, she had circumnavigated the globe twice. She 'never went dry', and was so valued that she was retired to 'a good English pasture for the rest of her life'. Dr Johnson wrote a letter about her to Cook's shipmate, Sir Joseph Banks (founder of Kew Gardens), including a Latin couplet:

PERPETUA AMBITA BIS TERRA PRAEMIA LACTIS,
HAEC HABET ALTRICI CAPRA SECUNDA JOVIS.

Johnson's biographer and friend, James Boswell, later translated this as:

IN FAME SCARCE SECOND TO THE NURSE OF JOVE,
THIS GOAT, WHO TWICE THE WORLD HAD TRAVERSED ROUND,
DESERVING BOTH HER MASTER'S CARE AND LOVE,
EASE AND PERPETUAL PASTURE NOW HAS FOUND.

Incidentally, a goat once saved the life of a baby aboard ship. The sloop Swallow was fighting an action in 1812, when Joseph Phelan, an able seaman, was mortally wounded on deck. His wife was assisting the ship's surgeon, but she rushed to her husband's side when she heard the news. As she was cradling Joseph in her arms, she was decapitated by enemy fire. The Phelans' shipmates took care of their three-week old son, and used milk from the officers' Maltese goat to feed the unfortunate orphan, who survived the ordeal.

One of the main objectives of Captain Cook's third voyage (1776–80), which turned out to be his last, was to find the theoretical North West Passage via the Pacific Ocean. Sadly, he failed, as did Captain Sir John Ross (1777–1856), although Ross did discover the Magnetic Pole. Ross's voyage was financed by his friend, the GIN magnate Felix Booth (1780–1850).

As well as gin, Booth was one of the first to see the commercial possibilities of GAS, and built the Brentford Gas Company (of which he was chairman) next to his distillery, to light the road between Brentford and Kensington.

The word 'gas' was invented in about 1600 by the Flemish chemist and physician, Jan Baptista van Helmont (1580-1644), and is said to be the single most successful invention of a word by a known individual in history. Other, less generous, souls say that it was in fact just his Belgian mispronunciation (and spelling) of the Greek word 'chaos', which is what he actually meant to call it.

Gin is made from grass. More specifically it's made of wheat or rye, which is 'malted' (meaning melted or softened) and flavoured with juniper berries. It was originally a medicine, invented in the Netherlands in about 1650 by Franciscus de la Boe, a medical professor at the University of Leiden. He called himself 'Dr Sylvius' (the Latinisation of his surname de la Boe, meaning 'of the woods') and he intended gin to relieve stomach complaints. But British soldiers serving in Holland soon found another use for it. They called it 'Dutch courage'. By the early eighteenth century, gin was the heroin of its day, causing terrible social problems, drunkenness and riots. Excise revenues tell us that, in 1733, eleven million gallons were distilled in London. By 1742, the figure was twenty million. (1 gallon = 3.78 litres *Ed.*) The Gin Act, passed in 1736, sought to put 'Mother's Ruin' out of the reach of the poor, by prohibiting the sale of quantities smaller than two gallons. However, in the first two years of the Act, 12,000 people were convicted of offences against it. This was good news for informants, who were rewarded for snitching on illegal gin shops.

One such nark was Captain Dudley Bradstreet, who later switched sides and set up the world's first slot machine since the time of the ancient Greeks. In his autobiography, he tells us he erected the sign of a cat by his ground-floor window. Passers-by would put money in the cat's mouth, and whisper 'Puss, give twopence worth of gin.' A lead pipe with a funnel at the end then dispensed a measure to the expectant dipso. In his first month's trading, Bradstreet raked in £220, a massive sum at the time.

Between 1710 and 1750, thousands of people died as a result of London's 'Gin Craze'. This wasn't merely because they drank seven (3.3 litres) or eight pints of it at a time. As well as containing alcohol and innocent juniper berries, the gin was often adulterated with turpentine and sulphuric acid.

Look out! Here comes the Fatha of the Railways...

GEORDIE STEPHENSON

and his softy son ROBBAT

WARNING!
This cartoon may contain traces of historical inaccuracy

George Stephenson was born in 1781 at Wylam in Northumberland, the son of a colliery fireman. He had no education, could not read or write, and at the age of 10 he began work in the colliery as a coal picker, sorting coal by hand to remove rocks and debris. George had a way with all things mechanical and repaired clocks as a hobby. He was soon given more responsible jobs looking after colliery pumps and winding engines. At the time of his promotion to enginewright, George was living in a small cottage with his sister Nelly and his young son Robert. Robert's mother, Frances, had died of consumption in 1806.

George's reputation spread and he was retained as an engineer by several colliery companies. In his spare time he invented a miners' safety lamp to help reduce the risk of explosions in mines, and tested it himself by walking into a mine filled with gas. When the celebrated scientist and would-be poet Sir Humphry Davy came up with a similar lamp, The Sunderland Society for the Prevention of Accidents in the Mines controversially awarded Sir Humphry Davy a £2000 prize for his design...

It was eventually proven that Stephenson's Geordie Lamp had been demonstrated to work prior to Sir Humphry's Davy Lamp. George was awarded a consolation prize of £1000 by a group of his supporters in Newcastle.

George Stephenson surveyed, drew up the plans and oversaw the construction of the entire railway. And when the Stockton & Darlington opened in 1825 – the first public railway in the world – George was at the controls of Locomotion, one of several engines he built for the line. However Stephenson did not invent the steam railway locomotive. Richard Trevithick had done that 21 years earlier at Pen-y-Daren in Wales. Stephenson had observed several pioneering locomotives at work in Northumberland, analysed their various designs and then set about improving upon them.

In 1823 George opened the world's first purpose-built steam locomotive factory near where Newcastle railway station stands today. He named the business Robert Stephenson & Co and gave his son the job of managing it. But trade was very slow to begin with, due largely to the fact that there weren't any railways yet to build locomotives for.

It was Robert Stephenson who took charge of designing and building the new locomotive while his father oversaw the building of the railway. However it was Henry Booth, the secretary and treasurer of the Liverpool and Manchester Railway, who came up with Rocket's most significant design innovation. Booth suggested using a multi-tubular boiler containing a large number of narrow copper pipes. This radically increased the heat exchange between the furnace and the water, and was to become a standard feature on all future steam locomotives. (A French engineer, Marc Seguin, had applied to patent a similar boiler design two years earlier.)

In October 1829, five pioneering locomotives lined up to compete for the £500 prize plus a contract to build engines for the Liverpool and Manchester Railway. On the final day of the Rainhill Trials a crowd of ten thousand turned up and witnessed the Stephensons' locomotive Rocket steaming to a clear victory.

Jolly Giraffe, Gray Jolliffe and Jeffy Gorilla
An out-of-depth scrutiny of

GENIUS

'Having the originality, intellect and imagination to think in hitherto unexplored areas and thus give mankind something of unique value it wouldn't otherwise possess.'

Encyclopaedia Britannica

 Ok you two. Let's get to the nub of this.

I'll start with Jung. Were it not for Jung's 'collective unconscious' my plane would still be on the tarmac. Passenger 'will power' alone got it in the air. Karl Jung was a genius. And the airlines agree.

Many people claim Freud was the genius.

Not in Jung's class! Jung could wipe the floor with Freud.

Whoa! Freud made a big comeback since neuroscientists proved him right about booze and cash having a direct effect on our emotions.

 But neither Jung's analytical psychology nor Freud's psychoanalysis could help James Joyce's daughter Lucia.

Joyce says that was because she was jung and easily freudened.

J.G. Ballard asserts that for the first time in 500 years there are no living geniuses.

Ballard?

Sounds like a duck with a head cold. How about Wayne Rooney?

He's no genius.

You didn't see the Croatia match.

Hummm... Better wind this up. But first, who are your personal favourite geniuses?

 Shakespeare. He produced all that stuff with a feather – clever or what?

Antony Worrall Thompson. If I could cook half that well I'd be one happy griller.

We only use one third of our brain.
British Medical Journal

 What do we do with the other third?

Thousands of geniuses live and die undiscovered by others, but mainly by themselves.
Mark Twain

Your mother is here to see you Mr Darwin

Nobody in football should be called a genius. A genius is a guy like Norman Einstein.
Joe Theisman

Only two things are infinite; the universe and human stupidity, and I'm not sure about the universe.
Albert Einstein

"I think they're for 1 a.m"
Descartes (preparing petits fours for an all night party)

Our curiosity about a thing is always obstructed by our preconceived ideas. The genius can see through that veil.
Theodore Zeldin

It's how the rockets go up, not where they come down, that's not my department says Werner von Braun.
Tom Lehrer

Your unconscious brain outweighs the conscious by ten million to one. Your brain is much smarter than you are, but only a genius will consult it.
Michael Gelb

💡 GENIUS in brief

ALBERT EINSTEIN was dyslexic, a womaniser and hated wearing socks. Even so, without him we would never have had the benefits of a curved universe, the atom bomb and nuclear power.

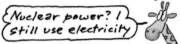

THOMAS EDISON invented the practical electric light. And for more than 70 years after his death he held the world record for the most patents. All this from someone who, aged 7, was expelled from school after only three months for being 'retarded'.

LEONARDO DA VINCI not only dreamed up the helicopter and the machine gun, but he was also handsome, a gifted musician and exceptionally strong. He could bend a horseshoe with his bare right hand.

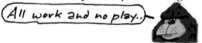

ISAAC NEWTON is the most important scientist in history and his *Philosophiae Naturalis Principia Mathematica* the single most important work in the history of science ever. But he was a mean, angry religious zealot who had no friends and probably died a virgin.

RICHARD FEYNMAN was a brilliant scientist and mathematician. Noted for his sense of humour, his work at Caltech had mainly to do with quantum physics and other arcane stuff like whether or not photons had mass.

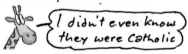

💡 GENIUS in fiction

There are lots of geniuses in fiction. Captain Nemo and Sherlock Holmes are two. Douglas Adams' paranoid android, Marvin, had four billion times the intelligence of any human but was lumbered with menial tasks and depression.

In *Catch 22* Milo Minderbinder was a crazy genius conducting business between both sides in the Second World War. 'Frankly' he said, 'I'd like to see government getting out of war altogether and leaving the whole thing to private enterprise.'

Although there have been many women who have made huge contributions to the sum of human knowledge and progress, not one has been hailed as a true genius. Historically this is because most were too busy giving birth to them. In popular lists of geniuses, Dolly Parton is the only woman who appears consistently, but no one really knows why.

A national poll of 4,000 Britons, to find the 100 greatest living geniuses (conducted in 2007 by global consultancy firm Creators Synectics) included: Damien Hirst (15=), Rupert Murdoch (20=), Osama bin Laden (43=), Richard Branson (49=) and, of course, Dolly Parton (94=).

On your drive, on the path and, er, in the gravel pits – it's all around you and life just wouldn't be the same without it. Welcome to the world of **gravel**!

But how much do you really know about this geological wonder?

Gravel spotting is often the first step in a life-long interest in gravel. Finding and sketching gravel in situ is cheap, healthy and fun and will allow you ample time to consider whether to invest in the more time-consuming (and expensive!) hobby of gravel *collecting*.

A gravel collection

Let's start with the basics: Is it gravel at all? If it's made of stone and its largest dimension is over 2 mm but less than 64 mm (2½ in) then – congratulations! - you've found gravel. Any bigger and it's a 'cobble' any smaller and, well, that's sand. (The word gravel actually comes from the Old French *gravelle* meaning 'coarse sand', which is a typically confusing French approach to things).

Not gravel

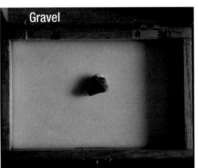

Gravel

Not gravel

Types of gravel: Gravel comes in all shapes and sizes (within the limits defined above). So let's look at some of the many fascinating types.

Bench gravel is found on the side of a valley, indicating a former, higher level for the river. It is a type of 'plateau gravel'. The first proof that mankind was millions (not thousands) of years old came when Boucher de Perthes (1788-1868) discovered both flint tools and the bones of extinct animals in the same bench gravel beds in Abbeville, Northern France.

Creek rock is the name for the water-smoothed gravels dredged from rivers and streams, mainly for use in concrete. It was extensively studied by the geographer Stanley Beaver (1907–84), whose work was vital in locating gravel sources for the building of RAF airfields in the Second World War.

Crushed rock, also known as 'Fool's Gravel' is pretend gravel made by crushing rocks. Careful not to be taken in! In 1912, Charles Dawson (1864–1916) hoaxed the archaeological establishment when he presented the skull of the first known

'missing link' between apes and humans to the Geological Society of London. He claimed to have 'discovered' it at a (real) gravel pit near Piltdown in Sussex. Known as The Piltdown Man, the forgery was actually made of the jaw of an orang-utan and some chimpanzee teeth glued onto a human skull, but this was not finally accepted until 1953, more than 30 years after Dawson's death.

Crushed stone is another 'false gravel' (usually pulverised limestone) used in road surfaces. The only really collectable form of this is granite Dense Grade Aggregate (DGA). You may hear 'pro' gravel collectors refer to this as 'crusher run'. Worldwide, many

more roads are surfaced with gravel than concrete or tarmac. Russia alone has over 400,000 km (249,000 miles) of gravel roads. In Australia, 10 mm (0.39 in)-sized crushed stone is called 'blue metal' despite being neither blue nor made from metal.

Fine gravel, often preferred by the ladies, is defined as having a long axis no greater than 2 mm, leading to some enthusiasts claiming it is really coarse sand. When the fine gravel is removed from a sample what is left is known as 'lag gravel', often preferred by lags.

Pay gravel is perhaps the king of gravels and is the preserve of the wealthy gravel collector. It is gravel that is rich in precious metals, making it suitable for mining and particularly for gold panning. It's where the term 'hitting pay dirt' comes from.

Pea gravel is the ideal starting point for the new gravel collector. It consists of small rounded stones often used in garden paths and aquaria. Archaeologists can sometimes deduce the location of ancient buildings by the accumulation of pea gravel in an area. Sir Arthur Conan Doyle (1859–1930) modelled Sherlock Holmes

on Joseph Bell, his mentor at Edinburgh University Medical School. Bell would impress his students with his study of the minutiae of evidence – such as gravel on the sole of a shoe, indicating the route a patient had taken to work.

Piedmont gravel is coarse gravel swept down by mountain torrents and deposited on plains. It is a type of 'river-run gravel' - that is, any gravel found in or near a river. Deep-sea diver William Walker (1869–1918) saved Winchester Cathedral from collapse between 1906 and 1911. The building, which rested on wooden foundations in a marsh, had began to sink. 235 holes were cut into the sodden ground, which rapidly filled with water. Wearing a full diving suit, Walker plunged into these holes to reach the solid river gravel, 8 metres (26 feet) below the surface. On the gravel he methodically placed 25,000 bags of cement, 115,000 concrete blocks and 900,000 bricks. Working in total darkness, he did this for 6 hours a day for 5 years. Every weekend, he cycled 240 km (150 miles) back home to see his family in Croydon.

Gravel is another name for bladder and kidney stones, the solid concretions formed in the body from minerals dissolved in the urine. In Wrexham, Wales on 7th August 1740, the poet Jane Brereton (1685–1740) died after a 5-week attack of 'the gravel.'

Grose Indecency

English has traditionally excelled as a FILTHY LANGUAGE. For centuries, Britons were RENOWNED for their inexhaustible ability to be rude in all sorts of colourful ways.

But in these days of POLITICAL CORRECTNESS GONE MAD, the rich traditions of British MUCK have been progressively watered-down. Thanks to NANNY-STATE DO-GOODERS and Brussels bureaucrats, only twelve insults or nicknames are now legal, and none of these are allowed on the BBC at all.

Come with us back to the Golden Age of Rudery, when the rumbustious fruitiness of our native tongue was still in full flood, when you only had to walk down the street to have some MUTTON-MONGERING LULLY TRIGGER call you a quiffing rantallion.

So don't be a gullgroper, put down your gaying instrument and let's teach the gotch-gutted grumbletonians that WE'VE HAD ENOUGH of their rum-gagging!

Captain Francis Grose (1730/1 1791)

As with many people in the 18th century, we don't know exactly when Francis Grose was born, but he was baptised on 11th June, 1731. The son of a wealthy Swiss jeweller who had moved to London, he started his working life as a teenage soldier, serving in Flanders, fighting smugglers in Kent and retiring from the army at 21. He was Richmond Herald of Arms in Ordinary from 1755 to 1763 – a position bought for him by his father – and was made a captain in the Surrey Militia in 1778. But Captain Grose wasn't cut out to be either a soldier or a herald; he was to flourish as an artist, satirist, historian and lexicographer. An amiable man of extraordinary diligence, he began writing at the age of 40, publishing torrents of his work in instalments. His popular *Antiquities of England and Wales* (1772-76) was followed by the satirical *Advice to Officers of the British Army* (1782), then *Antiquities of Scotland* (1788-91), *A Provincial Glossary, with a Collection of Local Proverbs, and Popular Superstitions* (1787) and *Rules for Drawing*

Caricatures: with an Essay on Comic Painting (1788). He had just begun *Antiquities of Ireland* when he died suddenly of an apoplectic fit. Grose liked to eat rich foods and to drink port. He also liked to tell stories. An enormously fat man, he took great pleasure in the pun linking his name to his size. One of his best friends was Robert Burns who wrote in his letters that he had 'never seen a man of more original observation, anecdote and remark'. Today, Grose is best known for *A Classical Dictionary of the Vulgar Tongue* (1785), a collection of street slang, much of it deliciously foul-mouthed. The book was compiled by Grose and his appropriately named assistant Tom Cocking on midnight walks through London, where they would pick up choice vocabulary in slums, drinking dens and dockyards, adding them to their 'knowledge-box'. Taken together, *A Classical Dictionary of the Vulgar Tongue* and *A Provincial Glossary* define some 9,000 words then in common usage – all of which Dr Johnson had managed to miss out of his more famous *Dictionary of the English Language* (1755).

'Bum brusher?'

'Ballocks!'

Are you a member of the teaching profession?

Indeed not, I am a clergyman.

BUM BRUSHER and FLAYBOTTOMIST were both slang words for a teacher, i.e. one who regularly caned bottoms. BALLOCKS: As well as its better known meaning, 'ballocks' is an old slang word for a parson. In 1977, this piece of obscure and apparently useless information came in rather handy for Mr Christopher Seale, manager of the Virgin Records store in Nottingham. He was arrested by a policewoman for displaying the album Never Mind the Bollocks, Here's the Sex Pistols in his window, and charged under the Indecent Advertising Act, 1899. (The display was 2.74 m/ 9 ft long and the word BOLLOCKS appeared in letters 10 cm/4 in high). At Nottingham Magistrate's Court, John Mortimer QC, defending, called as an expert witness the Reverend James Kingsley, Professor of English at Nottingham University and a former Anglican priest, who gave a comprehensive history of the word bollocks and its various uses, after which the magistrates, while wholeheartedly deploring the situation, acquitted the defendant of all charges.

‘*Do you play the purser's pump, sir?*’ ‘*No, I'm a pricklouse.*’ ‘*I'm as queer as dick's hatband.*’

Do you play the bassoon, sir? **No, I'm a tailor.** **I'm not feeling very well, but I don't know why.**

Purser's pump: The Purser was the Supply Officer on a naval ship: one of his jobs being to supervise the rum ration. The rum was drawn out of the cask by inserting a syphon into the bunghole in the top. This was known as a purser's pump because it wasn't a pump: pursers, in charge of all food and drink aboard, were derided as cheapskates. *Purser's logic* is 'false economy'; a *purser's dip* is an undersized candle; a *purser's grin* is a sneer; a *purser's loaf*, a ship's biscuit; a *purser's medal*, a food stain on clothing. The curved mouthpiece of a bassoon somewhat resembles a syphon. **Pricklouse:** Contemptuous word for a tailor (one of many). Tailors, like pursers were deemed to be mean – and also effeminate. There was an old saying 'nine tailors make a man'. Grose reports that one London tailor, ordered to provide 'half a man' to the local militia, asked how that could possibly be done. He was told: 'by sending four journeymen and an apprentice'. Other insults for tailors were 'botch' (for obvious reasons) and 'woodcock' because of their 'long bills'. 'Pricklouse' is from the tailor's imagined pernickety assaults on individual vermin with his needle. Samuel Pepys records his wife angrily calling him a pricklouse in his diary. **Dick's hatband:** Until recently this was a very common expression on both sides of the Atlantic. It appears in many forms – 'tight as Dick's hatband', 'twisted as Dick's hatband', 'crooked as Dick's hatband' etc – but no one really knows where it comes from. A popular story has it that the phrase commemorates Richard Cromwell who took over control of England when his father Oliver died, but was not really up to the job. The 'hatband' is a humorous reference to the 'crown' that sat so uncomfortably on 'Dick's' head. Known as Tumbledown Dick or Queen Dick for his indecisive character, he was deposed after less than nine months in 1659. If the derivation is true, it's odd that the first person to record it in print was Francis Grose himself, 126 years later.

‘*I dine with Duke Humphrey!*’ ‘*Come polish a bone with me! My tits can spank us to town where I'll sluice your gob.*’

I'm too poor to eat. **Let me buy you dinner. My horses will take us merrily into town where I'll buy you a drink.**

Dining with Duke Humphrey: This ancient phrase relates to Humphrey, Duke of Gloucester (1390-1447), fourth and youngest son of Henry IV. A generous man, known as 'the good Duke', he kept an open house where anyone was welcome to drop in for dinner. When he died, 'to dine with Duke Humphrey' meant to go dinnerless, his hospitality having ceased at his death. In the 18th century, people with insufficient funds to pay their way at a meal would excuse themselves by saying they were 'dining later with Duke Humphrey'. This was a jokey reference to an aisle in Old St Paul's Cathedral where beggars gathered, named 'Duke Humphrey's Walk' because it was supposed to be near to the tomb of the good Duke. In fact, as Francis Grose pointed out in another of his books, *A Provincial Glossary* (1787), the tomb in question was actually that of John of Gaunt. Duke Humphrey is in fact buried in St Alban's Abbey. **Tit:** Originally applied to any small animal or object as in tomtit or titmouse, then to a horse, small for its kind or not fully grown, thence to any horse at all.

'I'm a prigger of prancers and I've been polishing the king's iron with my eyebrows.'

'You've had a norway neckcloth too, I'll be bound, and you'll be scragged, ottomised and grin in a glass case.'

I'm a horse-thief and I've been in prison.

And in the pillory too, I imagine. You're going to end up being hanged, dissected and your skeleton exhibited at Surgeon's Hall.

POLISHING THE KING'S IRON WITH MY EYEBROWS: i.e. looking out of metal-barred windows, whilst detained at His Majesty's Pleasure. NORWAY NECKCLOTH: A pillory was a device for public humiliation and physical (sometimes lethal) abuse. It had hinged wooden boards with holes cut into them, into which the victim's head and hands were inserted, after which the boards were locked together. The timber for pillories often came from Norway spruce trees. SCRAGGED: To be scragged was to be hanged by the neck until dead. The scrag-end of lamb or veal is the thinner and scrawnier part of the neck.

'I popped a tatler in the urinal of the planets!'

'A busnapper seized my rammer and ramped my munster plums!'

'Are you a flaybottomist?'

'No, I'm a fartcatcher.'

I pawned my watch in Ireland!

A constable grabbed my arm and forcibly took away my potatoes!

Are you a teacher?

No, I'm a footman.

TATLER: A tatler or tattler was originally a striking watch, i.e. one that made a noise to mark the hour - and comes from the word tattle (1481) meaning 'to prattle'. Today, tattler is black American slang for an alarm clock. URINAL OF THE PLANETS: It rains a lot in Ireland. The equivalent insult for Scotland was 'Louse Land'. BUSNAPPER: To 'buzz' someone was to pick their pocket, so 'a buzz' is a pickpocket. To 'nap' or 'nab' is to catch, steal or seize, so a busnapper or buzz-nabber is someone who catches pickpockets, in other words a constable. FLAYBOTTOMIST and BUM BRUSHER, as we've indicated earlier, were both slang words for a teacher, i.e. one who regularly caned bottoms. FARTCATCHER: Footmen were known as 'fartcatchers' because they walked behind their master or mistress in the street.

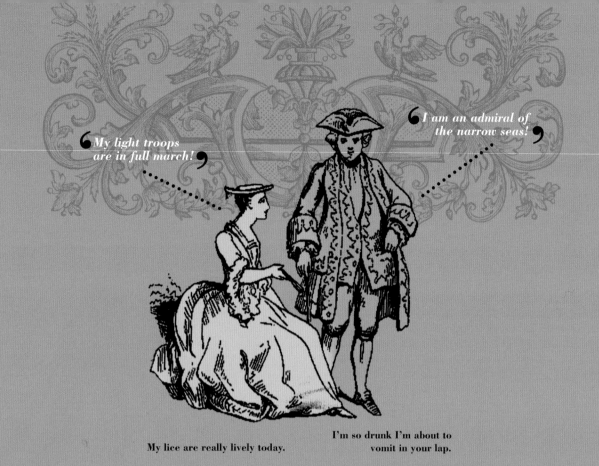

'My light troops are in full march!'

'I am an admiral of the narrow seas!'

My lice are really lively today.

I'm so drunk I'm about to vomit in your lap.

ADMIRAL OF THE NARROW SEAS: Whereas an 'admiral of the narrow seas' is a drunk whose vomit sails across the narrow gulf between his mouth and his neighbour's lap, a 'vice admiral of the narrow seas' is one who urinates into his companion's shoes under the table.

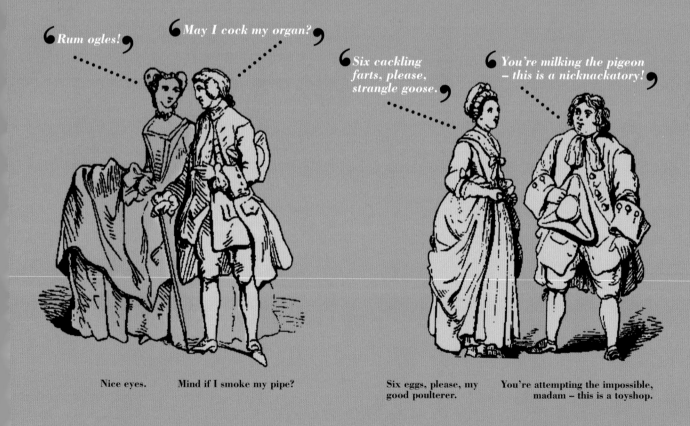

'Rum ogles!'

'May I cock my organ?'

'Six cackling farts, please, strangle goose.'

'You're milking the pigeon – this is a nicknackatory!'

Nice eyes.   Mind if I smoke my pipe?

Six eggs, please, my good poulterer.

You're attempting the impossible, madam – this is a toyshop.

RUM OGLES: 'Rum' was 16th century slang for 'fine' or 'excellent', it only came to mean 'strange' in the late 18th century. Ogles were eyes, from which we get the verb 'to ogle'. COCK MY ORGAN: The cock of a gun is the lever raised and brought down by the trigger. In old firearms, this brought a lit match into contact with the gunpowder in the flash pan, which then exploded firing the ball. To 'cock a gun' was to place a match into the appropriate part of a matchlock. Hence, 'to cock' a pipe was to light it. Pipes of the smoking kind were nicknamed organs as a pun on their pipes of the musical kind.

GIRAFFES

The Eleven Most Commonly Asked Questions (probably)

1. WHY DON'T GIRAFFES FAINT?

You might expect them to, when you see them raise their heads up from ground level - a distance of around 5.5 metres (18 feet) - in just a couple of seconds. Luckily, they have very high blood pressure, and are wise enough not to take tablets for it. Their legs are covered in tight skin that prevents blood pooling, and have strong muscles to pump it rapidly brainwards. It's long been thought that their jugulars contain a series of check valves to prevent sudden light-headedness. Latest research, however, suggests that the real key to the giraffe's anti-fainting mechanism is simply the massive size and power of its heart, which makes up 2.3 per cent of its body mass, compared to 0.5 per cent in humans.

2. DO GIRAFFES EVER FEEL FAINT, THOUGH?

Very probably. Mathematical models show that when a giraffe has its head at floor-level to drink, and then raises it suddenly in response to potential danger, it takes nearly ten seconds for normal blood-flow to be restored. In other words, say scientists, 'Giraffes feel faint when startled.'

3. WHY AREN'T GIRAFFES' NECKS LONGER?

Typically, a giraffe's neck accounts for half of the animal's total height. Even taller would be even better, perhaps - but the size of heart required to service it would, it is thought, be entirely unfeasible. The factors potentially affecting evolution are of course limitless ... but who'd have guessed that the avoidance of fainting was one of them?

> I know who I am. No one else knows who I am. If I was a giraffe and somebody said I was a snake, I'd think 'No, actually I am a giraffe.'
>
> **RICHARD GERE**

4. WHO WAS THE TALLEST GIRAFFE EVER, AND SHOULD I CARE?

George, an inmate of Chester Zoo in the 1960s, is said to be the tallest known captive giraffe, at just under 6 metres (20 feet). And you should care because even the dullest piece of trivia hides an interesting story.

For years, the zoo's telephones kept going down, and the engineers couldn't figure out why. It turned out that big George was licking the wires on the telegraph poles, causing them to (ha-ha!) short. He also stole visitors' hats. George knew, as Gandhi did, that resistance takes many forms.

5. WHAT'S THE ONE THING EVERYONE KNOWS ABOUT GIRAFFES?

That they never lie down, other than to die. But of course, they do. Conservationists at Oakland Zoo, California, note that: 'They often lie down to sleep, with head and neck lying across the flanks, although these sleeping periods tend to be brief - one to twenty minutes.' That's a long way down, for 60 seconds of shut-eye.

6. WHAT DO GIRAFFES DO FOR FUN?

Same as you, my friend: they drink. In the wild, splaying their legs and lowering their heads to drink makes them vulnerable, and they avoid it: they can go without water for longer than camels can. But in captivity, when water is provided at a convenient height, they will drink and drink and drink ... not from necessity, but for pleasure.

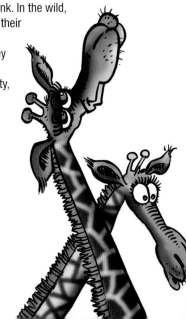

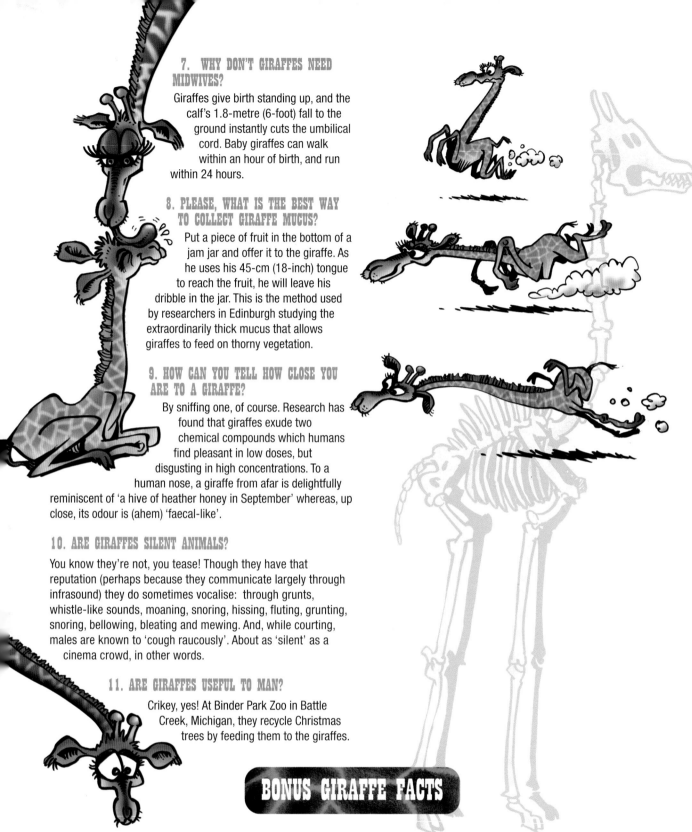

7. WHY DON'T GIRAFFES NEED MIDWIVES?

Giraffes give birth standing up, and the calf's 1.8-metre (6-foot) fall to the ground instantly cuts the umbilical cord. Baby giraffes can walk within an hour of birth, and run within 24 hours.

8. PLEASE, WHAT IS THE BEST WAY TO COLLECT GIRAFFE MUCUS?

Put a piece of fruit in the bottom of a jam jar and offer it to the giraffe. As he uses his 45-cm (18-inch) tongue to reach the fruit, he will leave his dribble in the jar. This is the method used by researchers in Edinburgh studying the extraordinarily thick mucus that allows giraffes to feed on thorny vegetation.

9. HOW CAN YOU TELL HOW CLOSE YOU ARE TO A GIRAFFE?

By sniffing one, of course. Research has found that giraffes exude two chemical compounds which humans find pleasant in low doses, but disgusting in high concentrations. To a human nose, a giraffe from afar is delightfully reminiscent of 'a hive of heather honey in September' whereas, up close, its odour is (ahem) 'faecal-like'.

10. ARE GIRAFFES SILENT ANIMALS?

You know they're not, you tease! Though they have that reputation (perhaps because they communicate largely through infrasound) they do sometimes vocalise: through grunts, whistle-like sounds, moaning, snoring, hissing, fluting, grunting, snoring, bellowing, bleating and mewing. And, while courting, males are known to 'cough raucously'. About as 'silent' as a cinema crowd, in other words.

11. ARE GIRAFFES USEFUL TO MAN?

Crikey, yes! At Binder Park Zoo in Battle Creek, Michigan, they recycle Christmas trees by feeding them to the giraffes.

BONUS GIRAFFE FACTS

A giraffe's heart is 2 feet (0.6 m) long and weighs about 25 pounds (11 kg).

A giraffe's tongue is 18 inches (45 cm) long and almost as dextrous as a hand. It's a purpley-grey, blue-black colour, supposedly to prevent sunburn.

A giraffe's neck, like that of almost all mammals, has only seven bones in it. A hummingbird's neck, like that of most birds, has 14.

Poachers kill giraffes for the metre-long tufts of hair on the end of their tails, which are cut off for making into bracelets. After the tail is removed, the dead giraffe is simply abandoned.

Some African tribes treat nosebleeds with the smoke from burning giraffe skin, whereas others have found that their leg-tendons make excellent bowstrings.

More than half of all giraffes do not live to be more than six months old.

Giraffes are notoriously accident-prone and unintentionally dangerous. Being tall they fail to see tents, tread on them, and then panic and start thrashing about.

Giraffe hooves are the size of soup-plates.

In 2002, anxious to examine its hooves for incriminating evidence, police pursued a giraffe suspected of murdering Father Karaffa, an American priest, by trampling him to death in a Kenyan game park. But, after an hour-long chase, the animal committed suicide by jumping off a cliff.

What Use is a Goose?

As 80s pop sensations *Frankie Goes to Hollywood* once remarked: 'War - What is it good for? Absolutely Nothing!' The same could be said about geese, except for the fact that they are... er... really very useful indeed.

BUT BEFORE YOU RUSH OUT AND BUY A FLOCK, **just exactly what can you do with geese?**

HERE ARE 15 HELPFUL SUGGESTIONS:

1. EAT ONE

Roast goose is traditionally eaten in Germany on Martinmas (11th November) in memory of Saint Martin of Tours, who, according to legend, hid in a barn full of geese to avoid being made a bishop, until the geese gave him away with their honking. He is the patron saint of geese.

2. EAT ANOTHER ONE

Goose is also traditionally eaten in Britain at Michaelmas, the Feast of St Michael the Archangel, on 29th September. According to legend, this came about because Queen Elizabeth I was tucking into goose when she heard of the defeat of the Spanish Armada in 1588, and so ordered that goose be eaten on that day every year to commemorate the event. Sadly, this is nonsense. In 1588, the tradition was already at least 100 years old and, in any case, the Armada was defeated in August. According to Jane Austen, eating goose on Michaelmas Day ensures that you won't be short of money in the following year. She tried this just before the publication of the second edition of *Pride and Prejudice*. It worked for her.

3. GO ON, HAVE A THIRD, YOU KNOW YOU WANT TO

Goose has always been popular for Christmas dinner in Britain. It was Henry VIII who first came up with the idea of turkey instead. In Charles Dickens' *A Christmas Carol*, the Ghost of Christmas Present shows Scrooge a vision of the Cratchits eating goose for Christmas dinner but, after Scrooge has mended his ways, he orders a more fashionable turkey for them. Dickens doesn't say what happened to the Cratchit's goose. Lord Byron was in the habit of buying geese to fatten them up for Christmas but became so attached to them that he couldn't kill them. He ended up with four pet geese. Until the 19th century, Christmas geese were walked to London from East Anglia in flocks over 1,000 strong. With their feet dipped in tar and sand as makeshift walking boots, they managed a brisk nine miles a day.

4. STUFF THEM AND STUFF YOURSELF

The discerning goose gourmet will salivate at the mere thought of *pâté de foie gras* – made from the swollen livers of geese, force-fed with grain through a metal tube – although over 95 per cent of French *foie gras* is now made with duck liver instead. This is much kinder to the geese. You can now also get 'ethical' *foie gras* from Spain, where the geese are plumped up slowly and voluntarily and then only lightly killed. The wartime recipe of pig's liver and potato casserole was known as 'poor man's goose'.

5. SERVE THEM AS FISH

For centuries it was mistakenly thought that geese hatched from the barnacles washed ashore on driftwood - hence the names *barnacle geese* and *goose barnacles*. Because such geese were never seen in summer, it was assumed they bred underwater (rather than, as we now know, in the Arctic). As a result, some Catholic dioceses allowed them to be eaten during Lent because they were 'fish'. In 1215, Pope Innocent III banned this absurd practice as it was patently silly. About as ridiculous, in fact, as translating the Bible into French... which he also banned.

6. SLEEP WITH THEM

Goose is an old slang term for 'prostitute'. The prostitutes of medieval Southwark came under the protection of the local landowner, the Bishop of Winchester, and so were known as 'Winchester geese'. 'Goose' also became a common name for venereal disease. 'Gooseberry bush' is 19th century slang for pubic hair – which is why babies are found under it.

Right: Menage à trois including Goose.

A GOOSE BETWEEN TWO FOXES.

7. PLAY A ROUND WITH THEM

Early golf balls were made of goose feathers enclosed in a leather ball and were known as 'featheries'. From 1848, these were superseded by latex 'gutties' made from the rubbery sap of the *gutta percha* tree.

8. DOODLE WITH THEM

Penna is Latin for 'feather', and is where we get the word 'pen' from. *Quink*, the world's top-selling ink, is also an old name for a Brent Goose. When writing with quill pens, right-handed people used feathers from the left wing of the goose, and vice-versa.

9. SWEEP CHIMNEYS WITH THEM

Geese were used by Irish chimney sweeps in the 19th century. Inserted into the fireplace, they'd try to fly up the chimney, beating their wings in a tremendous panic, dislodging soot as they went.

10. SWEEP ACROSS EUROPE WITH THEM

The goose step, called in German *Der Stechschritt* (or 'prick-step'), was an early 19th century Prussian invention, later adopted by the Imperial Russian Army. Contrary to what you imagine, the Nazis actually phased it out very early on in the Second World War: after 1940 it was no longer taught to new recruits. But it's still used today in the Russian Federation, North Korea, Cuba, Vietnam, Chile and Iran – and in China, where slow goose-stepping soldiers presented the Olympic flag at the 2008 Beijing Games.

Above: 'A first lesson in the Goose Step' by W. Heath Robinson

11. INSTALL THEM AS A BURGLAR ALARM

According to legend, in the 4th century BC, a flock of sacred geese famously saved Rome by squawking an alarm during a stealthy night attack by the Gauls. It's less well known that, since 1959, Ballantyne's Whisky warehouses on the Clyde have used a flock of 70 guard-geese known as 'the Scotch Watch' to protect their stock. Quite interestingly, geese don't get goose-bumps when they're frightened.

12. GET THEM TO DO THE WEEDING

Many farmers in the USA employ 'weeder geese' to keep orchards and fields clear of unwanted vegetation. For some reason, geese eat grass and weeds voraciously, but leave the valuable crops – strawberries, coffee, cotton, Christmas trees, onions, asparagus, tobacco – completely alone. Only geese do this. Working from dawn to dusk, they root out weeds that are inaccessible to tools or machinery, and which would otherwise have to be expensively hand-weeded or poisoned with noxious chemicals.

13. GET THEM TO HELP WITH THE COOKING

Geese make excellent kitchen skivvies – there are several 19th century accounts of them turning spits, using their powerful necks like an arm.

14. KEEP ONE NEXT TO THE FIRST AID KIT

Geese offer an organic alternative to Bonjela for treating mouth ulcers, as detailed in this account from 1881: '*A goose was brought to the little patient's side, and the bird's head was thrust into the child's open mouth, and held there for about five minutes, for nine successive mornings. By that time the inflammation of the mouth had disappeared.*' A goose-bill is also a type of forceps used for removing bullets.

15. WIPE YOUR BOTTOM WITH THEM

Geese make superb, fully-recyclable soft toilet paper* (especially if you've run out of puppies), as the great French Renaissance writer François Rabelais (1494-1553) records in *Gargantua* (1534):

'I have, by a long and curious experience, found out a means to wipe my bum, the most lordly, the most excellent, and the most convenient that ever was seen. I wiped my tail with a hen, with a cock, with a pullet, with a calf's skin, with a hare, with a pigeon, with a cormorant, with an attorney's bag, with a falconer's lure.

But of all torcheculs, arsewisps, bumfodders, tail-napkins, bunghole cleansers, and wipe-breeches, there is none in the world comparable to the neck of a goose that is well downed, if you hold her head betwixt your legs. For you will thereby feel in your nockhole a most wonderful pleasure, both in regard of the softness of the said down and of the temperate heat of the goose.'

*Toilet paper as we know it today was only invented in 1902, at the Northern Paper Mill at Green Bay, Wisconsin. However, it wasn't until 1935 that they were finally able to advertise it as 'splinter-free'.

65

Gordons
by Clive 'Son of a Gordon' Anderson

GORDON IS A MORON was a one-hit wonder for Jilted John in 1978. My father's name was **Gordon**, and though the lyrics make it clear that the **Gordon** in the song has many impressive qualities (better looking, cooler and trendier than Jilted John, at any rate), in my family the repeated phrase *Gordon is a Moron*, caused us much amusement. The song includes the line 'I was so upset I cried all the way to the chip shop' - making it the second best British hit single to mention the classic British takeaway after Kirsty McColl's *There's A Guy Works Down The Chip Shop Swears He's Elvis.*

The expression (and the song) *Gordon is a Moron* have come back into vogue since **Gordon** Brown went from Greatest Chancellor Of All Time to Worst Prime Minister In Living Memory about as fast as it takes to get from No. 11 to No. 10 Downing Street. His first name is actually James but the use of his second name **Gordon** avoids confusion with James 'Sex Machine' Brown whose showbiz career began entertaining troops at Camp **Gordon** in Georgia. **Gordon** Brown's father was a Church of Scotland Minister, which makes **Gordon** a 'son of the manse'. Many Scottish politicians and public figures are sons of the manse, but where in England are the sons of the vicarage? **Gordon** Brown lost the sight of his left eye (and very nearly the right as well) in a school Rugby game.

Another one-eyed **Gordon** is **Gordon** Banks, OBE, England's greatest goalkeeper. He lost his right eye in a car accident in 1972, putting a stop to his sporting career. Gordon Banks played every game in the legendary 1966 World Cup, but his most memorable save was against Brazil in the 1970 World Cup in Mexico, when he kept out a header by Pele. His biggest *mistake* as a goalkeeper was to eat whatever it was that upset his stomach before the quarter-final game against West Germany in the same tournament. Peter Bonetti took his place and England lost 3-2. Things might have been different had Banks been between the posts. In fact, England might even have had a second World Cup victory to bang on about.

The classified football results on BBC Radio have, for 35 years, been graced by the voice of James Alexander **Gordon**. His clear delivery and subtly weighted emphasis give the simple list of names and numbers a familiar, comforting rhythm. His pronunciation is so admired in Sweden that tapes of his work are used to teach English to university students. One thing you can't tell from James Alexander **Gordon's** voice is that he contracted polio as a baby, was in and out of hospital until he was 15 years old and still walks with a limp. As a child, he had a serious speech defect but he overcame it by immense and prolonged effort. His mother said the only time she had ever seen her husband cry was the day his son did his first radio broadcast. 'The wee bugger's done it!' he exclaimed.

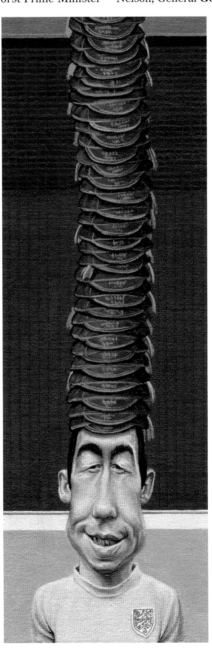

The most famous historical **Gordon** is **Gordon** of Khartoum. Like General Custer, King Harold or Admiral Nelson, General **Gordon** is doomed to be remembered for his last, lost battle, rather than his earlier exploits. In his lifetime he was known as Chinese **Gordon**, a war hero who led his 'Ever Victorious' army in China in the 1860s, returning loaded with honours from the Emperor. Visiting Brussels in the 1880s, **Gordon** so impressed the King of the Belgians that he gave him the job of running the Congo. Sadly, it was not to be. The British needed **Gordon** in the Sudan. Khartoum was under threat from a revolt led by the so-called 'Mad Mahdi', Mohammed Ahmed, and **Gordon's** job was to evacuate civilians to safety. This he did with great success, holding out against the Mahdi for more than a year before he was cornered, killed and beheaded, just two days before the British relief expedition reached the city to help him.

Gordon was a Christian evangelist who believed in reincarnation: he was looking forward to another life. He also believed that the Earth was surrounded by a sphere on which God's throne hovered directly above Jerusalem, with the Devil at the opposite point over Pitcairn Island in the Pacific.

'**Gordon** Bennett!' This useful euphemism, which sounds like a swearword but isn't, is thought to be named after James **Gordon** Bennett Jr, the American playboy son of James **Gordon** Bennett Sr. Gordon Bennett Sr was originally from Scotland, and left his son a fortune and the *New York Herald* newspaper. In his mid-20s **Gordon** Bennett Jr became engaged to the socialite Caroline May. At a grand New Year's party to celebrate the occasion in 1877, **Gordon** Bennett got so drunk he peed in the fireplace in front of his prospective parents-in-law.

His fiancée broke off the engagement and her brother gave **Gordon** Bennett a public horsewhipping.

Nowadays, perhaps, we should really cry out '**Gordon** Ramsay!' after the hugely talented chef who is as well known for his profanity as his profiteroles. **Gordon** Ramsay claims he was once on the books of Rangers Football Club. If only he had met Delia Smith early on, he could have been taught not to be so excitable while explaining cooking on telly, and played for Norwich City as well.

Gordon Ramsay advertises **Gordon**'s Gin, invented in Clerkenwell, London in 1769, by a Scot called Alexander **Gordon**. According to legend, his recipe is still used today: a secret formula known only to 12 people at any given time. Strangely, in these days of global branding, **Gordon**'s Gin is sold in green bottles in Britain but in clear glass bottles everywhere else in the world.

The amusingly titled Scottish dance 'The Gay **Gordons**' is named after the **Gordon** Highlanders, the tough regiment originally raised by the Duke of **Gordon** of Clan **Gordon** in 1794. The word gay had a rather different meaning when the **Gordons** were first called it. The word is probably a corruption of 'gey', an old Scottish term for hostile or ferocious. Or perhaps they just looked good in their kilts.

In the late 18th and early 19th century, Elizabeth **Gordon**, Countess of Sutherland, and her husband, the Marquis of Stanford, were the largest landowners in Britain. A Countess in her own right, Lady **Gordon** is chiefly remembered for the dreadful clearances of the Highlanders from her Sutherland estates in 1807- 21.

Oddly enough, **Gordon** County, Georgia – though a long way from Camp **Gordon** where James Brown learned to dance – roughly corresponds to the last stronghold of the Cherokees before they were forced out of their traditional hunting lands in 1850.

67

g-g-g-gags
NICK NEWMAN

'We think he's going to be a ventriloquist.'

'Death, War, meet Global Warming.'

'Genesis? I don't Adam and Eve it!'

'I advertise golf sales, but it's my day off.'

'It was either this or teaching.'

'I'm going to conserve energy and not vote.'

'Oh no! Gypsies!'

'Do we have to have giraffes?'

'Sorry to have kept you waiting – now what seems to be the problem?'

69

A girl should be two things:
classy and fabulous.
COCO CHANEL

The whisper
of a pretty girl
can be heard
further off than
the roar of a lion.
ARABIAN PROVERB

Girls

BY JACQUELINE BISSET

It's the good girls who keep diaries;
the bad girls never have the time.
TALULLAH BANKHEAD

I never cared
for fashion much, amusing little
seams and witty little pleats:
it was the girls I liked.
DAVID BAILEY

Put your hand on a hot stove for a minute and it seems like an hour. Sit with a pretty girl for an hour and it seems like a minute. That's relativity.
ALBERT EINSTEIN

Even today, well brought up English girls are taught by their mothers to boil all veggies for at least a month and a half, just in case one of the dinner guests turns up without his teeth.
CALVIN TRILLIN

I never expected to see the day when girls would get sunburned in the places they do now.
WILL ROGERS

As soon as she can stand, a girl searches out what is hidden. ALGERIAN PROVERB

There is no such thing as an ugly girl; there is, however, such a thing as not enough vodka. RUSSIAN PROVERB

ARE YOU A GUINEA GENIUS?

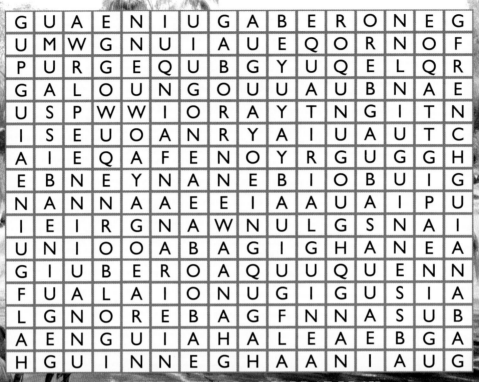

G	U	A	E	N	I	U	G	A	B	E	R	O	N	E	G
U	M	W	G	N	U	I	A	U	E	Q	O	R	N	O	F
P	U	R	G	E	Q	U	B	G	Y	U	Q	E	L	Q	R
G	A	L	O	U	N	G	O	U	U	A	U	B	N	A	E
U	S	P	W	W	I	O	R	A	Y	T	N	G	I	T	N
I	S	E	U	O	A	N	R	Y	A	I	U	A	U	T	C
A	I	E	Q	A	F	E	N	O	Y	R	G	U	G	G	H
E	B	N	E	Y	N	A	N	E	B	I	O	B	U	I	G
N	A	N	N	A	A	E	E	I	A	A	U	A	I	P	U
I	E	I	R	G	N	A	W	N	U	L	G	S	N	A	I
U	N	I	O	O	A	B	A	G	I	G	H	A	N	E	A
G	I	U	B	E	R	O	A	Q	U	U	Q	U	E	N	N
F	U	A	L	A	I	O	N	U	G	I	G	U	S	I	A
L	G	N	O	R	E	B	A	G	F	N	N	A	S	U	B
A	E	N	G	U	I	A	H	A	L	E	A	E	B	G	A
H	G	U	I	N	N	E	G	H	A	A	N	I	A	U	G

1: PURE GUINEAS WORDSEARCH

WORDS TO FIND: GUINEA — PAPUA NEW GUINEA — EQUATORIAL GUINEA — GUINEA-BISSAU
GUINEA PIG — GUINEA FOWL — GUINEA WORM — GUINNESS — HALF-GUINEA — GHANA — GUYANA
FRENCH GUIANA — GABON — GABORONE — GOLBORNE

2: RIDDLE-ME-RE

My first is in Guinea, but not in Bissau
My second's in Guinea and in Guinea fowl

My third is in Guinea and isn't in Ghana
My fourth is in Guinea and also Guyana

My fifth is in Guinea and also in Guinea
It's also in Guinea, and Guinea and Guinea

My last is in Guinea but isn't in pig
If you can't get the answer then you're a bit thick.

3: HOW WELL DO YOU KNOW YOUR GUINEAS?

1. This country contains half the world's bauxite
2. This is the only Portuguese-speaking country in the world with a Muslim majority
3. This is the world's third most aid-dependent country
4. Around a tenth of this country's population are refugees from neighbouring countries
5. This country has more recorded orchid species than any other country in the world
6. This country has more languages than any other in the world
7. This country has the fastest growing GDP on Earth
8. This is the only Spanish speaking country in Africa

4: MATCH THE COUNTRY TO THE FLAG

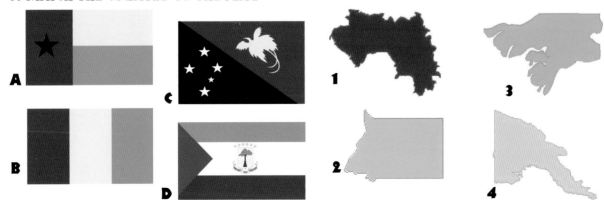

A
B
C
D

1
2
3
4

THE SUDO-N'KO

The official language of the ten million people of the Republic of Guinea in West Africa is French, but each of the 24 ethnic groups in the country also has its own language. These are known as the Mandé group of languages, from Maan-Den meaning 'Children of the Kings'. In the 1940s, Solomana Kante (1922-87), a Guinean nut merchant, became annoyed that his countrymen were seen as 'cultureless' because all their languages were oral and had no written alphabets. This was an ancient difficulty, first recognised more than 700 years earlier at a conference summoned by Sunjata, Emperor of Mali, in 1236. For seven years, Kante wrestled with the problem, experimenting for four years with an Arabic script and three years with a Latin one, before deciding that neither would do. According to legend, the solution came to him after a night of deep meditation and, on 14th April 1949, he unveiled his unique N'ko script to the world. N'ko – also known as The Clear Language – means 'I say' in all Mandé languages and is now used by 27 million people around West Africa.

THE QI SUDO-N'KO IS LIKE A NORMAL SUDOKU, BUT YOU MUST COMPLETE THE GRID SUCH THAT EACH ROW, EACH COLUMN AND EACH 3x3 BOX CONTAINS THE DIGITS 1-9 IN THE N'KO ALPHABET:

9	8	7	6	5	4	3	2	1

For solution to QI Sudo-N'ko please visit www.qi.com

g-g-g-gags

'Where do you stand on gay priests, God?'

'So much for omniscience'

'I suppose we'd better put an announcement in The Bible'

73

A dodgy cartoon of *Graham Norton* (with Les Dennis' hair) presents

GOLDEN GRAHAMS

A garrulous gander at some of my more notable

(Nothing to do with the popular breakfast cereal of the same name)

Hey baby I'm your telephone man?

Probably the most famous Graham in the history of the world is Alexander 'Graham' Bell (1847-1922), but he wasn't a proper Graham. As a child he was christened plain Alexander Bell. For some reason, unlike his two brothers - one older, one younger – his parents had neglected to give him a middle name. As a child he went on and on about this so, on his 11th birthday, his father allowed him to adopt Graham as his middle name... though everybody went on calling him Alec.

Graham's Crackers

Graham is the 30th most common surname in Scotland. Given a choice, however, Jocks tend to leave it well alone. In 2008 it failed to make the Top 100 boys' first names, trailing behind perennial Scottish favourites like Aaron (7th), Kayden and Muhammad (joint 82nd) and Noah (88th). The name originates from Grantham, in Lincolnshire, which is referred to in the *Domesday Book* as Graham. It means either 'grey home', 'gravel area' or 'Snarler's village'.

No, it's not a 3-D pool table...

....it's an orrery!

George Graham (c.1674-1751) was the Master of the Clockmakers' Company and a fellow of the Royal Society. Born into a poor farming family in Cumberland, Graham was to become the greatest instrument maker of his age, and partner of the famous watchmaker Thomas Tompion. Graham provided John Harrison with advice and a loan which enabled him to build his first marine chronometer, and many claim that (with Tompion) Graham built the world's first orrery - a mechanical model of the solar system - commissioned by (and named after) Charles Boyle, 4th Earl of Orrery. He also used precision clocks to measure the exact shape of the earth.

MASTICATION NOT MASTURBATION!

Feeling a tad frisky today? Fancy a bit of rough-age? Then get your teeth into this!

Sylvester Graham (1794-1851) was a dietary reformer who invented the Graham Cracker in 1829, and laid the foundation for modern-day breakfast cereals. A Presbyterian preacher, fanatical teetotaller and vegetarian, he recommended hard mattresses, cold showers and a diet of fruit, vegetables and home-baked bread made from unsifted, coarse-ground wheat. A bit of a cracker biscuit himself, he believed that an unhealthy diet containing meat and factory-baked bread would lead to alcoholism and excessive sexual urges. Graham's views caused some controversy, and during a visit to Boston in 1837 he was almost attacked by an angry mob of butchers and bakers.

Brothers' Oporto port package did not portend well

Ehhm... Excuse me! I think this looks more like Paul Daniels than me!

W. & J. Graham, makers of the world famous Graham's Port, only got into the wine trade by accident. In 1820 two brothers, Albert and John Graham, working for the family textile business, were sent to open an office in Oporto, Portugal. While there they accepted 27 pipes (3,105 gallons) of port wine in settlement of a bad debt and shipped it back to their head office in Glasgow. Initially reprimanded for not sending cash, Graham's port quickly proved more popular than Graham's textiles, and W. & J. Graham have never looked back.

Graham's Crackers

TV evangelist William Franklin 'Billy' Graham was a regular golf partner of Presidents Eisenhower, Johnson and Nixon. (Not all at once, though.) By 2008 he had preached to an estimated 2.2 billion people.

George Rex Graham (1813-94) was the American publisher who founded *Graham's Magazine* in 1841. The magazine's first editor was Edgar Allan Poe, and it was in *Graham's Magazine* that Poe's short story *The Murders in the Rue Morgue* was first published. This is widely (although not universally) claimed to be the first ever work of detective fiction. Poe's successor as editor of *Graham's* was his staunch critic and bitter rival, Rufus Wilmot Griswold.

Boo! Hiss! Rufus sounds like a barrel of laughs, doesn't he?

74

'What knight lives in that castle over there?'

Am I a gnome or a leprechaun? Or Alan Shearer?

I beg your pardon...

Graham Stuart Thomas (1909-2003) was perhaps the most influential rosarian of the 20th Century. His books, beginning in 1956 with THE OLD SHRUB ROSES, helped restore the then wilting popularity of England's national flower. In 1975 Thomas received the OBE for his work as gardens advisor to the National Trust, and the yellow rose 'Graham Thomas' is named after him.

Comedy legend Graham Chapman died in 1989, one day before Monty Python celebrated its 20th anniversary. Chapman was cremated and his ashes kept by his lover David Sherlock until the Millennium, at which point they were scattered over Wales as part of a firework display.

Graham's Crackers

American choreographer Martha Graham (1894-1991) taught Kirk Douglas, Bette Davis, Liza Minnelli, Gregory Peck and Madonna how to dance. In 1998, *Time* magazine named her 'Dancer of the Century'. (Just ahead of the BBC's John Sergeant.)

This Graham's NOT so Golden...

MORE gunky I'd say!

Stop there, it's getting too silly!

Graham Bond (1937-74) sold fridges and encyclopedias for a living before becoming a musician. His band The Graham Bond Organisation featured the impressive rhythm section of Jack Bruce (bass) and Ginger Baker (drums), both of whom went on to form Cream with Eric Clapton. Bond, who was born illegitimately and adopted as a child, was convinced that Aleister Crowley was his real father.

Optometrist Robert Klark Graham (1906-97) became a millionaire after inventing plastic eye-glass lenses. But he is perhaps best remembered for his achievements in the field of bespoke wank banking. In 1980 he set up the Repository for Germinal Choice, a sperm bank for clever tossers. Graham believed that not enough brainboxes were having babies. His solution was to travel around the world asking Nobel Laureates and male geniuses if they fancied a quick five-knuckle-shuffle. He died in 1997 after falling in his hotel bathroom during one such mess-collecting mission. His pioneering sperm bank closed soon afterwards.

Slow down! You're putting the wind up me!

Kenneth Grahame (1859-1932) was Company Secretary at the Bank of England when his first book was published in 1895. *The Golden Years* was a collection of short stories about a family of orphaned children. Grahame invented the character Toad while making up bedtime stories for his son, Alastair. However *The Wind in the Willows* was not well received by publishers or critics, most of whom seemed to want more stories about orphans. In 1920 Grahame's son Alastair was found dead on a railway line at Oxford. After his son's death Grahame wrote no more stories.

Graham's Crackers

James Graham (1878-1954), 6th Duke of Montrose, invented the aircraft carrier. Well, sort of.

Bette Nesmith Graham (1924-1980) invented typewriter correction fluid. Born Bette McMurray, she married a Nesmith and was the mother of Monkee Mike. Fortunately for me, in 1969 she re-married a Graham. In 1979 she sold her Liquid Paper business to the Gillette Corporation for a whopping $47.5 million.

Thomas Graham (1805-69) invented the word 'gel'. He also discovered dialysis, founded the Chemical Society of London, and formulated the law of diffusion of gases, known as Graham's Law.

Graham Bartram is the only living Graham deemed worthy of a mention on my page! He is a vexillologist and vexillographer (he researches and designs flags). A Fellow of the Flag Institute (yes, there is one), he is also the author of *British Flags and Emblems*, and flag consultant to the British Government.

So, ehhm... which one's Rat?

Crambs! That's all we've got room for!

GNUS OF THE WORLD.

Gnus are a kind of antelope also known as wildebeest. There are two types of gnu: the White-tailed Gnu (Black Wildebeest) and the Brindled Gnu (Blue Wildebeest). White-tailed gnus are extremely rare and live in South Africa. They are extinct in the wild and only exist in game reserves.

Brindled gnus live in East Africa and aren't rare at all, outnumbering all the elephants, warthogs, giraffes, gazelles, zebras, impalas, lions and hyenas in the region put together. Once a year, over a million of them travel 3000 km from the Serengeti in Tanzania to Kenya's Masai Mara and back again. Every day they eat 7,000 tonnes of grass and drink enough water to fill five swimming pools.

GNUS FLASH

BLACK DAY FOR WILDEBEEST In June 2009, a baby black wildebeest was born at Newquay Zoo in Cornwall: the first white-tailed gnu to be born in the UK in decades. Sadly, he died of a stomach complaint after only 29 days.

HUMMMMMMMMMM

I heard you the first time.

GURU OF GNUS

HELLO GNU FANS

The world's leading authority on gnus is the American naturalist Richard Estes. His team collects wildebeest dung with a silver spoon and analyses it. He is also famous for finding a warthog scent gland shared by all other hogs in the world. It had gone completely unnoticed in the 7,000 years since pigs were domesticated.

Most of the year, male gnus bellow 'ga-noo' but, at the first full moon after the rainy season, they also start to hum – and this turns female gnus on. The Guru of Gnus describes it as "a basso profundo mating chorus" – a cross between lowing cattle and giant bullfrogs – that "rumbles like waves against a headland."
Hmmmm

The Guru of Gnu is trying to prove that it is this humming that causes all female gnus to become sexually receptive at the same time. Eight months later 500,000 calves are born within 3 weeks of each other. Predators have a field day – but can't eat as many as they would if the births were spread out. Gnuborn babies can stand within as little as 3 minutes and run with the herd from 2 hours after birth. In large herds, 80% of newborns survive the first month.

HAVE I GOT GUNS FOR YOU

RUBBISH

CLUCK CLUCK

Before guns came along, the sensible gnu hunter would put an ostrich's head on a stick and tuck some ostrich feathers into his loincloth. Gnus and ostriches often graze together & the disguise allowed hunters to approach to within spear range.

Matt's Gravity

LAST GRAVITATIONAL PULL FOR 238,000 miles

GRAVITY
ON
OFF

SIR ISAAC NEWTON DISCOVERS THE PRACTICAL JOKE

'I'm not overweight, I just suffer from overactive gravity'

MATT

78

Bill Bailey's Air Guitar Masterclass

STEP 1: First select your air plectrum.*

You are now ready to air guitar.
LET'S ROCK!

*This could be an imaginary Jim Dunlop 0.73mm, or a 1.0mm for maximum rockage.
Or a piece of stale naan bread. Or a tiddlywink.

STEP 2:
Try not to drop it.

STEP 3:
Place a lit cigarette upright in the headstock, preferably non-filter Gaulois etc. for bonus cool. Extreme caution advised (note the pinky raised in concentration).

STEP 4:
Warm up with some limp indie noodling. Don't go mental just yet, light strumming, and a gloomy demeanour.

STEP 5:
Bit more oomph now with some basic plucking. Here I'm demonstrating the classic Bert Weedon 'education can be fun' look.

Chord Positions

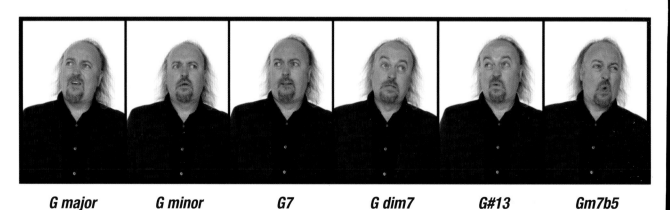

| G major | G minor | G7 | G dim7 | G#13 | Gm7b5 |

Photography by Andy Hollingworth

STEP 6:
*Now try a few rock leaps –
are you nimble enough for the
Hair-Metal Scissor?*

STEP 7:
*The Amp-Smash. Recreate the classic
by Kurt Cobain at Reading in '92.*

STEP 8:
*Rawwk! Screwed up eyes and screwed down
hairdo - like some cat from Japan!*

You have now completed Basic Air Guitar!

1. THE CLASSIC.
*This is the twiddly
middle bit from the
classic riff (and air
guitar standard)*

*Free's 'Alright Now'
(or any riff at any
time since guitars
were invented).*

2. THE HAMMER.
*This involves
banging the strings
onto the fretboard,
or 'hammering on'.*

*This technique is
often used by
guitarists when they
can't remember what
song they're playing.*

3. THE CRAB.
*Thumb and
forefinger remain
clamped to the
neck, while the*

*three others (the
Crab's Legs) can
scuttle freely –
good for jazz.*

4. THE LEMMY.

*5. THE VULCAN.
(Spock's Delight).*

6. THE CROCODILE.
*This was pioneered
by Chic guitarist Nile
Rogers. Due to his
classic see-through*

*guitar, he was able
to perform shadow
puppetry during Le
Freak to the delight
of the crowds.*

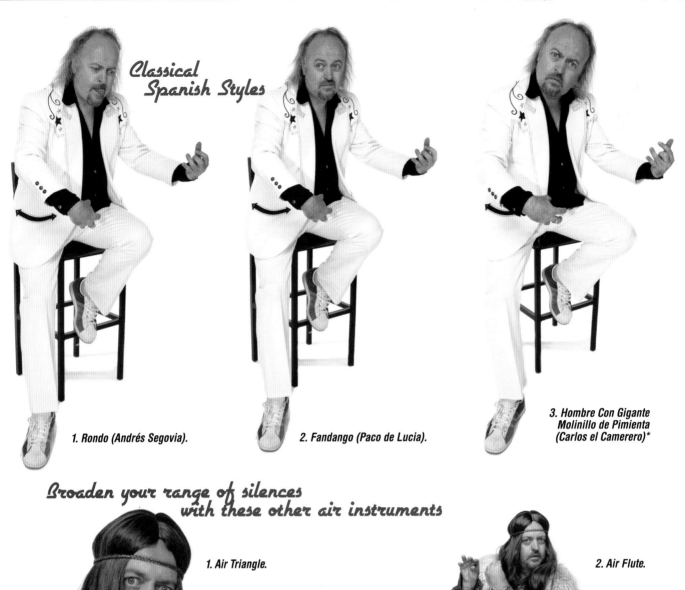

Classical Spanish Styles

1. Rondo (Andrés Segovia).

2. Fandango (Paco de Lucia).

3. Hombre Con Gigante Molinillo de Pimienta (Carlos el Camerero)*

Broaden your range of silences with these other air instruments

1. Air Triangle.

2. Air Flute.

4. Adjusting an Air Amp. (This one is a 1969 Marshall Master Lead Combo).

3. Air Sitar.

*Man With Giant Pepper-Grinder (Carlos the Waiter)

PHIL JUPITUS
radio 4 idea machine

HELLO CHUMS... HAVE YOU EVER WANTED TO SUBMIT IDEAS FOR SHOWS TO RADIO FOUR? IT'S EASY! ALL YOU HAVE TO DO IS WHAT I DO! JUST TAKE THE EXISTING SCHEDULE AND ADD THE LETTER G... THESE SHOWS WILL MAKE THEMSELVES!

"THE GNUS QUIZ"

SANDI TOKSVIG ENTERS A WORLD OF TOPICAL WHIMSY WITH 4 WILDEBEEST...

"FEEDBAG"

ROGER BOLTON IS FORCE FED A LARGE BAG OF OATS...

"GROSSING CONTINENTS"

VARIOUS BBC FOREIGN CORRESPONDENTS TRY TO FEED PEOPLE BRITISH FOOD AROUND THE WORLD...

"SHIPPING GORECAST"

GUTS, MOVING SLIGHTLY... OCCASIONAL BLOOD, SOME PUS...

LEADING SURGEONS DESCRIBE OPERATIONS AS THEY PERFORM THEM TO NAUSEOUS SAILORS...

"THE ARGHERS"

AAARGH AAARGH

A SIMPLE TALE OF COUNTRY FOLK WHO SCREAM AT EACH OTHER FOR NO REASON...

"THE GEEK IN WESTMINSTER"

I'M A TENTH LEVEL WARLOCK

AN I.T. CONSULTANT AND DUNGEONS AND DRAGONS FAN IS FORCED TO DO AN INTERVIEW WITH POLITICIANS

"DEAD GINGERS"

WE REGRET TO ANNOUNCE THAT ANN ROBINSON IS NOT IN THE SHOW THIS WEEK

A PROGRAMME FEATURING VARIOUS DECEASED "STRAWBERRY BLONDES"...

"G.M."

sigh

EDDIE MAIR'S DNA IS MANIPULATED EVERY NIGHT AT FIVE O'CLOCK...

"GO 4 IG"

THE SCARY MAN HE HURTED ME...

EVERY WEEK A YOUNG LISTENER IS ENCOURAGED TO ATTACK IGGY POP THEY ARE INTERVIEWED IN HOSPITAL.

"LOOGE ENDS"

AH... YES WHEN IS YOUR BOOK OUT?

CLIVE ANDERSON IS TAKEN UP THE ALPS AND STRAPPED TO A TEA TRAY TO CONDUCT CELEBRITY INTERVIEWS AT SPEED...

"THE MORAL GAZE"

BASICALLY A NUN HYPNOTISM SHOW.

"QUST A MINUTE"

AND AS THE MINUTE WALTZ AAAAAAAAAAAAAAAAA

NICHOLAS PARSONS IS TAKEN INTO A WIND TUNNEL FOR HALF AN HOUR

"MUGGYBOX"

OOOH ITS HOT

THIS WAY UP

DO NOT OPEN

PAUL LEWIS IS NAILED INSIDE AN UNVENTILLATED CRATE AND FLOWN TO MUMBAI IN THE SUMMER

"GIN OUR TIME"

WHO WANTS SOME IT THEN

MELVYN BRAGG AND HIS PANEL OF GUESTS DRINK A CASE OF GIN AND HAVE A MASSIVE FIGHT...

"LAG IN ACTION"

HE WAS DREADFUL! I GOT SIX YEARS!

EX-CONVICTS GATHER IN THE STUDIO AND MOAN ABOUT THEIR CRAPPY LAWYERS...

"ANY ANGERS?"

JUST 'ANY ANSWERS' WITH A NEW NAME...

"GOO AND YOURS"

ENTIRE FAMILIES ARE COVERED IN CUSTARD FOR NO REASON...

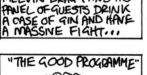

"THE GOOD PROGRAMME"

ENOUGH SAID...

"FROM OUR GOWN CORRESPONDENT"

KATE ADIE FORCES BBC JOURNALISTS TO WEAR DRESSES...

I'M SOGGY + HAVEN'T A CLUE

FOOOSH

BARRY CRYER, TIM BROOKE TAYLOR + GRAEME GARDEN ARE HOSED DOWN FOR 30 MINUTES...

gremlins: little known facts

The word 'gremlin' was first recorded in 1923.
It may come from the Irish gruaimin, 'a bad-tempered little fellow'.
The word 'fact' was first recorded in 1539. It originally meant 'an evil deed'.

A dietician writes:
The staple diet of the
Gremlin is Hot Snot
and Bogey Pie.

Roald Dahl reputedly
popularised the Gremlin legend
during the Second World War,
when gremlins were blamed for
inexplicable mechanical failures
in fighter aircraft. But their
reputation lives on and they have
recently been held responsible for
the sub-prime crisis and for MP's
expenses. 'That's correct',
said a reliable source.

FYI:
Sir Dahl lived in
a shed and wrote
popular stories
for children.
His father was an
Indian take-away
dish and his
mother couldn't
spell Ronald*.

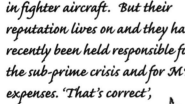

Gremlins are very
keen on staring
competitions and
will stare at you for
many days, possibly
even weeks, on end.

* Spelling mistake copyright Peter Spence, 1979

A baby Gremlin is called a 'heggessey'. The collective noun for Gremlins is a 'lorimer'.

A Gremlin will steal your braces at the most embarrassing time.

I dub thee, Sir Willie.

Gremlins at play.

Stephen Spielberg made a movie about Gremlins. 'It was hard work', one of Sir Spielberg's associates told our correspondent. 'They were pesky little creatures who kept breaking down the whole time. We used to blame them.'

Walt Disney first brought Gremlins to the cinema in the 1940s. Sir Disney originally dubbed his creations Michael and Donald Gremlin.

Is this true? – Ed.

Gremlin mashing potatoes.

Female Gremlin making off with a pizza cutter.

The GLOBAL GLEANINGS of GLANVILLE GLIBBTHORPE

Straight through the globe in 42 minutes and 12 seconds flat!

The biggest globe in the World is … the World!

And since the dawn of time Man has dreamed of digging a tunnel straight through the World and seeing where he comes out (go on, you know you have). So what's stopping him? Well, 40 miles[1] of rock for starters, followed by 8,000 miles[2] of white-hot magma for the main course, and then another 40 miles[1] of rock for pud.

It's easy to imagine that you might run over budget on a project like that.

But a man can have a dream, can't he? Here's mine: we've dug a tunnel from London to Sydney. We've built a frictionless train to run through the tunnel. For good measure, we've pumped all the air out of the tunnel so there's no wind resistance. Now all we need to know is: how long will it take us to get to Australia?

And here's the weird part: we know the answer, and we know it *exactly*, because it was worked out by Isaac Newton and his pen-pal Robert Hooke, 350 years ago. Here's what they figured: once your gravity train starts down the tunnel it'll fall like a jet-propelled stone. You'll pass the centre of the Earth doing 17,670mph[3], but then you'll start to slow down, until you reach the other end of the tunnel – where you'll stop, and then go all the way back again to where you came from, like a ball thrown into the air and falling back to earth. And those two old brain-boxes calculated how long each one-way trip would take: you'd go clear though the planet in 42 minutes and 12 seconds – exactly.

But suppose your tunnel didn't go right through the middle of the Earth? Suppose it went to New York, or Beijing, or Buenos Aires or somewhere. What then? This is the even weirder part: whichever two points on the surface of the Earth you tunnelled between, the trip would take exactly the same time: 42 minutes and 12 seconds.

Realistically, it's not going to happen – there's just too much white-hot gunk in the way and, frankly, you may as well go by plane. **BUT:** on the *Moon*, it might be a different story. There's no molten core, no atmosphere, and no damn nimbys to tell you to go build your tunnel someplace else. So maybe the gravity train will be viable for real there one day. If so, here's another bit of weirdness. The Moon is only 2,000 miles[4] across, a quarter of the diameter of the Earth – but the trip would actually take longer there: 53 minutes, in fact. **Put *that* in your pipe and smoke it!**

A Global Perspective from the Inside

Here's a problem with any Globe you care to name: whatever you do, you can't see more than half of it at a time. Or can you? An MP and geographer named James Wyld hit upon the answer in 1851, when he built a 60-foot[5] tall scale model of the Earth in London's Leicester Square – which could be looked at *from the inside*. All the land- masses and mountains and rivers were modelled in plaster of Paris on the inside surface of the sphere, lit by gas and viewed by Victorian visitors from platforms in the middle of the display. It was a popular attraction for eleven years. Sadly, in 1862, the lease on the land expired and it had to be demolished.

Apparently, everyone who visited Wyld's Globe loved the way it gave a truly accurate impression of the whole world all at once, simply by turning it outside-in. Curiously enough, you can make a mathematical model of the entire Universe inverted in this way: if we were living on the inside of a globe then the Sun would be 2.5[6] metres in diameter and every other star would be contained within a radius of 1mm[7] of the centre.

Now, much as I'd like to, I don't claim that we actually are living on the inside of the globe – but there have been people who really did think so. In the 1890s, Dr Cyrus Teed of New York convinced a substantial number of followers that they were doing just that – with the Sun, Moon and stars all floating in the middle of this huge sphere. Dr Teed built a device called a 'Rectilineator' to measure the curvature of the surface of the sea, and concluded that it was, sure enough, concave – which proved that he had been right all along!

The Globe Theatre

The Shakespearean theatre on the south bank of the Thames in London isn't globe-shaped and never was.

The modern version is a twenty-sided polygon, but it isn't a replica of the Elizabethan structure, as nobody knows quite what that was like. In fact, it's known to differ in a number of respects: the location is different for one thing. For another, in Elizabethan times the timbers would have been whitewashed – the dark timbers that we associate with Tudor buildings nowadays would appear distinctly odd to a Tudor time-traveller.

The original Globe burnt down on June 29th 1613 when a cannon being used on stage set the thatched roof alight. Only one person was hurt: a man whose britches were set on fire. He sorted himself out by pouring his ale on them.

A Globe of Salford

The globally respected presenter of the popular QI TV show once told a funny story about a man who went into a shop and said he wanted to buy a globe. They offered him a range of globes of the Earth, but he said he wanted a globe of Salford. Cue much laughter in QI-land. but it turns out that the laugh is on them, because 'Globes of Salford' really do exist; they are collectible old bottles with a globe logo on them, made by Groves and Whitnall of Salford. Wrong again, clever-clogs so-called QI Gnomes!

Well, that's the end of this glimpse into the glorious globe-tastic world of globes. Keep it global!

FOOTNOTES: 1: 64.3 km – Ed. **2:** 12,800 km – Ed. **3:** 28,272 kph – Ed. **4:** 3,200 km – Ed. **5:** 18.3 metres – Ed. **6:** The same size as the gilded globe on top of St Saviour's church in Copenhagen, just big enough to accommodate 12 grown men – Glibbers. **7:** Absolutely tiny – Glibbers.

Your pal,
Glanville Glottthorpe

Glossoplegia

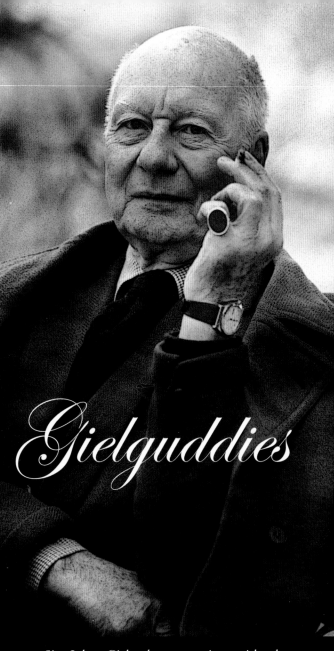

Gielguddies

Sir John Gielgud was eating with the playwright Edward Knoblock when an acquaintance walked past their table. '*Thank God he didn't stop,*' said Gielgud. '*He's a bigger bore than Eddie Knoblock… of course I don't mean you, Eddie.*'

Gielgud once remarked to Elizabeth Taylor: '*I don't know what's happened to Richard Burton. I think he married some terrible film star and had to live abroad.*'

Gielgud went to see Richard Burton in his first performance of *Hamlet* at the Old Vic and afterwards went backstage to take him out to dinner. The dressing room was packed, so Sir John shouted over the crowd: '*I'll go ahead, Richard. Come along when you're better – I mean, when you're ready.*'

Lunching with the theatre critic Kenneth Tynan who'd just seen a new play called *The Joint*, Gielgud asked what it was about. Tynan said: '*It's about a masochistic convict who keeps getting imprisoned because he likes being fucked by sadistic negro murderers.*' '*Well,*' said Sir John, '*You can't quarrel with that!*'

What is a pachyderm packing in its pants?

If they did wear underpants, African bull elephants would surely struggle to find any large enough to house their humungous happy lamp. For between their legs they maintain the largest love lighthouse of any land animal, with a penis measuring a metre or more in length. Their jumbo testes are located internally, as a pair of dangling bollocks weighing around 2 kilos (4lb 6oz) each would have an adverse effect on even the most agile elephant's gait. Each nad has a cubic capacity equivalent to that of a large football. A cow elephant's vagina measures 70 to 90 centimetres in length, and her clitoris a whopping 40 cm. Scientists believe that, because of their tusks, elephants don't do oral.

Genital Knowledge Quiz Question:

How do you MASTURBATE an elephant?

As tugging away at their cocks would be both dangerous and unproductive, when mammologists need to collect elephant sperm for insemination, one unfortunate individual has to shove their arm right up the animal's bottom and vigorously stimulate its prostate gland, while a colleague positions himself strategically... with a bucket.

Fuck a duck!

Most birds don't have dongs, but the Argentine lake duck definitely does have! For the drake is blessed with what genital experts are calling 'the Swiss army knife of knobs'. The duck's retractable multi-purpose corkscrew-style cock extends to a full-length of half-a-metre (17 inches). Duck cock experts speculate that these wondrous wangs act like a lasso for apprehending reluctant partners, and that their soft, brush-like bell ends might be used as a 'womb broom' to remove a competitor's sperm from the female's oviduct prior to ejaculation.

The human equivalent in terms of body length to penis size ratio would be a man with a six-foot chopper!

Let's look at... GIANT GENITALS

A focus on the fascinating world of very big reproductive organs

Words Charlie Cheaplaugh
Pictures Tom Tracing-Paper

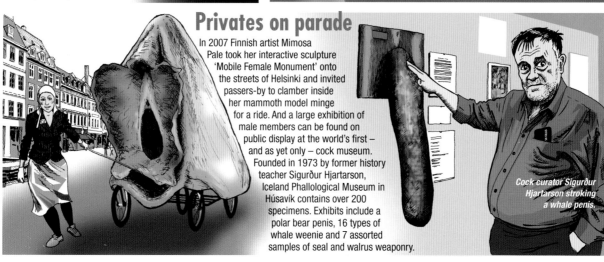

Monsters of the deep

The largest testicles known to man are those of the right whale (also known as the Greenland whale, great whale or black whale) each knacker weighing in at 500kg (or 1,100lb). That's equivalent to the combined weight of Sir Elton John, at his least trim, playing a Steinway model D concert grand piano. But any underwater explorers hoping to catch a glimpse of these colossal conkers will be disappointed. Because like all other cetaceans, the whale keeps the family jewels tucked safely away inside.

Sir Elton John and barnacle's cock not drawn to scale

The unlikely king of the underwater cocks is the barnacle. In gentle waters barnacles develop long, flexible fun truncheons for greater reach. Those living in rougher water have shorter schlongs. A barnacle's John Bobbitt can grow up to eight times its body length, the longest trouser snake - relative to body size - of any animal.

Privates on parade

In 2007 Finnish artist Mimosa Pale took her interactive sculpture 'Mobile Female Monument' onto the streets of Helsinki and invited passers-by to clamber inside her mammoth model minge for a ride. And a large exhibition of male members can be found on public display at the world's first – and as yet only – cock museum. Founded in 1973 by former history teacher Sigurður Hjartarson, Iceland Phallological Museum in Húsavík contains over 200 specimens. Exhibits include a polar bear penis, 16 types of whale weenie and 7 assorted samples of seal and walrus weaponry.

Cock curator Sigurður Hjartarson stroking a whale penis.

How big was King Kong's dong?

It's the question which has been baffling cinema audiences ever since the original King Kong movie was released in 1933. And at last we have a definitive answer. Throughout the movie Kong's height varies, from 18 feet when he is discovered on Skull Island, to 60 feet during some scenes in New York. Kong's creator Merian C. Cooper, who wrote the original story, envisaged Kong being '40 to 50 feet tall'. But his fluctuating size on screen was due to animator Willis O'Brien and his crew who manipulated the giant ape's height by varying the scale of the miniatures and altering camera angles during the filming of special effect sequences.

A full-size bust of Kong used during the filming had been built in scale with a 40 foot ape, while RKO Pictures' promotional materials listed Kong's official height as 50 feet. Based on that official figure we can reveal that King Kong's dong would have measured a rather disappointing 13.7 inches – *on the bonk*. And his testicles would have weighed less than two cricket balls.

Real gorillas grow to about 5 feet 8 inches tall (1.7 metres) yet achieve an erection length of less than 2 inches! Their testes together weigh only 30 to 35 grams.

Giant toss-up between biggest cocks

Fish experts cannot say with any certainty which whale has the world's largest whanger. Both the right whale and blue whale are estimated to have 3 metre (10 foot) whalehoods. So it's a massive toss up for first prize. Three metres might seem impressive to a passing dolphin, but taking into account the blue whales' overall size – they can grow to a length of 30 metres (98 feet) and tip the scales at 180 tonnes – their 3 metre member is the equivalent of a human wielding a 10 centimetre pork sword.

How a big dick compares

MASSIVE

BIG

QUITE BIG

SMALL

TINY

UNITS OF WHALE COCK MEASUREMENT

At 1.85 metres in height Cristiano Ronaldo (right) is dwarfed by a blue whale's whanger.

Dino rods shrouded in mystery

Despite having museums stuffed full of dinosaur bones, paleontologists haven't got a clue how big their prehistoric boners used to be. However, the chances are they had a small vent tucked beneath their tail – a cloaca, like those of modern birds and reptiles – and whatever wedding tackle they did have at their disposal would be kept in there. On a more positive note, paleontologists can tell us that the world's oldest surviving penis is the 425-million-year-old fossilised member of an ocean-dwelling ostracode crustacean discovered in England during 2003 by scientists from Leicester University. They named it *Colymbosathon ecplecticosis.* Translated from Latin this means 'amazing swimmer with a large penis'.

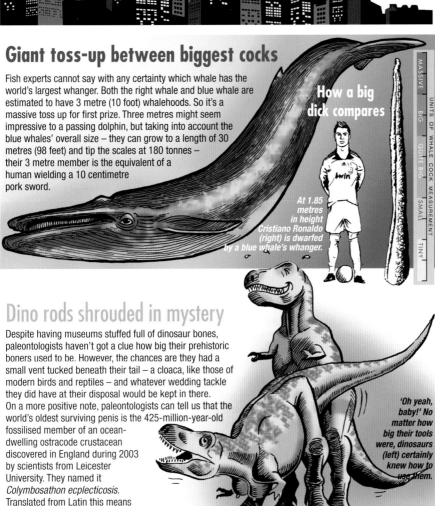

'Oh yeah, baby!' No matter how big their tools were, dinosaurs (left) certainly knew how to use them.

Giant's beanstalk

The Cerne Abbas Giant, carved into a hillside near Dorchester in Dorset, stands 180 feet tall and has a giant beanstalk measuring 30 feet from the tip of its bell end down to its biffin bridge. Local tradition has it that a giant was slain on the hillside and that the villagers of Cerne Abbot drew around his body to create the giant outline. That, with all due respect, is another big load of bollocks. The figure may represent the god Hercules and be of Iron Age or early Roman origin. But more recent research suggests that the giant carving, cut in the form of narrow trenches in the turf in order to expose the chalk below, may date from the 15th Century and be the work of an irreverent local land owner. Lord Denzil Holles, who owned the site between 1642 and 1666, was a fierce critic of Oliver Cromwell and the chalk man may have been designed to satirise Cromwell's puritanical ideals.

Nigel's cock was too big

The biggest cock ever recorded measured an incredible 64 feet in length! But it didn't belong to a whale, a dinosaur or a giant monster from the movies. It was a massive metal monstrosity created by Sir Nigel Gresley, Chief Mechanical Engineer of the the London and North Eastern Railway. Gresley's gargantuan, powerful, rigid-bodied P2 class steam locomotive *Cock o'the North* was designed to *pound* up the steep gradients, *pump* its way around the shapely curves and *plunge* its streamlined front end deep into the moist, steamy tunnels of the Edinburgh to Aberdeen railway line. Built at Doncaster in 1934, *Cock o'the North* weighed 167 tons and had eight massive driving wheels, each measuring over 6 feet in diameter. Unfortunately due to track damage caused by its weight, over-heated *big ends*, hot *boxes* and the fact that some platforms were simply not big enough to accommodate the *Cock's* massive *load,* the engine was withdrawn in 1943 and rebuilt as a more manageable A2 class locomotive.

Sir Nigel Gresley, whose monstrous (if not somewhat tenuously defined) 'cock' was far too big.

GILFS
Goats I'd Like to Farm

BY SEAN LOCK, RETIRED GOATHERD

Although I am now a national celebrity and multi-millionaire*, I have always been a simple goatherd at heart.
Here's my tribute to my beloved former colleagues from those happy days of my youth in Creuse, France

1: Goat Basics:
When goat-herding there are really only two things you need to bear in mind:

1. There is nothing wrong with going to bed with someone of your own sex. People should be very free with sex, but they should draw the line at goats. SIR ELTON JOHN

2. By candlelight, a goat looks like a lady. FRENCH PROVERB

2: Goat Identification:
This is definitely a goat.

This looks quite like a goat, but isn't.

3: Goat Facts:

Ω There are about 480 million domestic goats in the world.

Ω China has far more goats than anywhere else: approximately 197 million of them. French gentlemen travelling to the Orient who are not of Sir Elton's persuasion should remember to carry a powerful torch.

Ω Goat soup is the national soup of Liberia. It is served at all important state functions.

Ω The ancient Greek word 'tragomaskalos' means 'with armpits smelling like a he-goat'. In Japan, you can get goat's milk and goat's meat-flavoured ice cream.**

Ω George Orwell had a pet goat called Muriel. She appears as a character in 'Animal Farm' – as the only animal that can read.

Ω A python can open its mouth wide enough to swallow a goat whole, but this is not good for either of them. The goats don't enjoy it at all and the pythons often die from the strain.

Ω The Mau Mau terrorists of Kenya in the 1950s initiated their guerrillas by making them have sex with goats. Or so they say. Kenyan rebel strongholds in the 1950s were very dimly lit. It could have been an honest mistake.

This is an artist's impression of me, in my herding uniform. For dramatic licence, the mountains behind are actually in Kazakhstan. The scenery in Creuse is very different – rolling farmland, lush wooded valleys and goats, goats, goats.

FAMOUS PEOPLE WHO BEGAN AS GOATHERDS: Genghis Khan, Pope Clement IX, George Orwell, Me, Kaldi, the legendary Ethiopian boy whose goats first discovered coffee.***

Without my morning coffee I'm just like a dried up piece of roast goat.
J.S. BACH (1685-1750) The Coffee Cantata

* Oh yes, ha bloody ha. ** Ben & Jerry's once made a rose-flavoured ice cream. It was tested before going on sale but abandoned almost immediately after one person who tried it remarked 'This tastes like my grandmother's armpit.' *** Google it! I don't see why I should do all the work here…

Goat-related puzzles

Goats are highly intelligent and enjoy problem solving – which ledge to stand on, where to go for lunch and so forth. I've never actually seen one do a crossword, but there's a first time for everything (as the bishop said to the goat!!!!).

5: Goatdoku
Place goats so that every square below has a goat on it.

4: Goatword

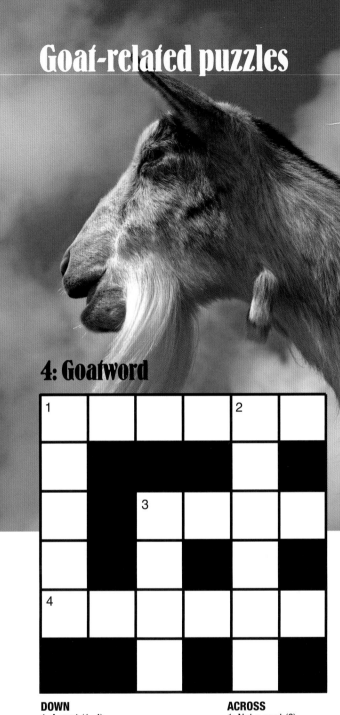

DOWN
1: A goat (1, 4)
2: (and 4 across) A cashmere goat (11)
3: Horned ruminant (4)

ACROSS
1: Not a goat (6)
3: Toga (anag.)
(Answers on page 98)

Mr Mountain Goat image courtesy of Frank Newman.

'She's doing porridge'.

'Oh no! Someone's invented gridlock!'

93

Gee-Kwiz!

GEOGRAPHY! *(Lots of forfeits in this round...)*

1. They don't ring The Lutine Bell (or 'a bell'). (MINUS 2)
The Lutine bell developed a crack and the practice of ringing news of lost ships has now ended. The last time the bell was used to announce the loss of a ship was in 1979 and the last time it rang a safe return was in 1989.

2. They don't have a siesta. (MINUS 2)
Less than half of Spaniards have a snooze in the afternoon. A study published in 2005 found Spaniards got an average of 40 minutes less sleep than the European average. Spanish men spend more time working or studying than their compatriots in Britain, Germany, Sweden and seven other northern European countries, a survey found.

3. It's not Liebfraumilch. (MINUS 2)
Liebfraumilch is made entirely for export. Most Germans have never even heard of it.

4. Hungary. (PLUS 2) **Not Italy.** (MINUS 2)

5. French Guiana or Guyane. (PLUS 2)
Guyane, a *Département* (DOM) of France, sends 2 deputies to the French National Assembly. One of them represents the largest constituency by land area in the French Republic.

6. Gabon. (PLUS 2)

7. There aren't any. (MINUS 2)
Uniquely, the Gulf of Gabes off the coast of Tunisia has an 8ft (2.4m) rise and fall.

8. The Metropolitan County of Greater Manchester. (PLUS 2) **Lancashire.** (MINUS 2)
Wigan has been part of the Metropolitan County of Greater Manchester since the Local Government Act, 1972.

The Lutine Bell

GARDENING!

1. Not Wales. (MINUS 2) **Asia.** (PLUS 2)
Welsh onions aren't native to Wales and have never been grown there to speak of. The word 'Welsh' is a corruption of Old English *welisc* and German *welsche* meaning 'foreign'. 'Welsh' onions originated in Asia: Chinese, Japanese and Korean all have their own words for them.

2. None of them are gooseberries. (PLUS 2)
They're all different kinds of shrub that resemble gooseberries or gooseberry bushes in some way. Chinese gooseberries are otherwise known as kiwi fruit.

3. A potato, which has 48, 2 more than humans. (PLUS 2)

4. Kew Gardens. (PLUS 2)
According to *Country Life* magazine.

5. 70,000. They're awfully small. (PLUS 2)

6. One. First name Boris. Pasternak is Russian for parsnip. (PLUS 2)

7. Garden hose, which he used to devise the first pneumatic tyre for his son's bicycle. (PLUS 2)

8. Not plums. (MINUS 2)
Dried grapes or raisins; sultanas, currants, almonds, figs, cherries, lemons, figs (2 POINTS FOR ANY OF THESE).

Pasternak (above); Dunlop (right)

G-MEN!

1. Garibaldi, Nice. (PLUS 2)
Garibaldi, the liberator of Italy, was born in what is now part of France. In those days, Nice belonged to the Duchy of Savoy, and was known as Nizza.

2. Gabor. (PLUS 2)
The nine husbands of Zsa Zsa Gabor (7 divorces, 1 annulment, I survivor) and Gábor Dénes aka Dennis Gabor, the British Hungarian inventor of the hologram and, incidentally, the flat screen TV in 1958, 30 years before Clive Sinclair. (His patent ran out in 1968 before it could be manufactured.)

3. Gandhi. (PLUS 2)
Quote is from Joe Morgenstern in the *Los Angeles Herald Examiner* (1983).

4. He was torpedoed (or drowned). (PLUS 2)
Pantaléon Enrique Granados y Campina (1867-1916) sailed to the US in 1916 to oversee the premiere of his masterpiece *Goyescas* at the New York Met. A White House summons to play for President Woodrow Wilson meant he missed his boat and, on his eventual way home to Spain, he and his wife were torpedoed and drowned.

5. Sir John Gielgud. (PLUS 2)
'I've dropped enough bricks to build another Great Wall of China.'
For more Gielguddies, turn to page 89.

6. The distinguished Arab playwright, Sheik Zubair. (PLUS 2) Actually it was a joke (and quite a good one), originally made in a speech in 1988, but it was printed in *Playboy* as if he'd meant it and widely reported as such in the British press.

7. Galileo Galilei. (PLUS 2) The year was 1564.

8. Gabriele D'Annunzio (1863-1938). (PLUS 5) D'Annunzio was an Italian nationalist playwright, poet and novelist. In 1919, with a small volunteer force, he occupied the town of Fiume, where he remained as dictator till 1921.

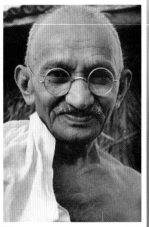

Galileo (left); Gandhi (centre) and the amazing hummingbird (above). Below, Jupiter's Great Red Spot.

GREATNESS!

1. Doris. (PLUS 2)

2. Bluetooth. (PLUS 2)

Gorm the Old began the Danish ruling dynasty. His son Harald Bluetooth succeeded him and completed the conquest of Denmark. Bluetooth's son was Sweyn Forkbeard and one of his grandsons, Canute the Great (1018-35) became a memorable King of England. The name Bluetooth was chosen to suggest Scandinavian unity.

3. Lincoln Cathedral. (PLUS 2)

For almost 300 years, from 1280 to 1549, Lincoln Cathedral was the tallest building in the world, its 525 ft/160 m tall spire overtaking the Great Pyramid. Though this collapsed due to bad weather in 1549, the cathedral kept the title till 1884 when the Washington Monument (555 ft 5⅛ in or about 169 m) was built.

4. Sir Winston Churchill. (PLUS TWO)

His son, John Churchill, the famous general, was created Duke of Marlborough by Queen Anne in 1702 – oddly enough before the victories for which he is remembered. His wife was a favourite of the Queen, but John had already been made Earl of Marlborough in 1689 by King William III.

5. Catherine the Great. (PLUS 2)

Like her grandmother-in-law Catherine I (a Lithuanian peasant christened Marta) she wasn't called Catherine and she wasn't Russian. She was Saxon. Zsa Zsa Gabor's present husband comes from the same family.

6. The Great Red Spot on Jupiter. (PLUS 2)

7. The swaddling clothes that wrapped the baby Jesus in the manger; the loincloth Christ wore at the Crucifixion; the Virgin Mary's cloak; the cloth that John the Baptist's head was wrapped in after he was decapitated. (PLUS 2 FOR EACH ONE)

8. The orrery. (PLUS 2)

A mechanical model of the Solar System. Commissioned by and named after Charles Boyle, 4th Earl of Orrery.

GENERAL IGNORANCE!

1. Five, including a silent one. (PLUS 2)

All can be seen in the phrase 'mighty rough garage gin'.

2. Ganymede, one of the moons of Jupiter. (PLUS 2)

Larger in diameter than the planet Mercury, it has only half its mass. It has the highest mass of all planetary satellites – twice that of the Earth's moon. Ganymede's discovery is credited to Galileo Galilei, who observed it in 1610.

3. Five. (PLUS 2)

The Milky Way, Andromeda, The Large & Small Magellanic Clouds and the Triangulum. They're not all visible from both hemispheres at once, and you need pretty good eyesight for a couple of them.

4. Herod the Great. (PLUS 2)

5. The Gateshead Millennium Bridge. (PLUS 2)

Linking Gateshead and Newcastle across the Tyne, it's the world's first, most energy efficient and (so far) only tilting bridge. It sits on 19,000 tonnes of concrete and cost £22 million to build.

6. Gas. (PLUS 2)

Van Helmont also invented the word 'blas' (meaning astral radiation) but it didn't catch on. Unlike gas. Even George W. Bush knows what that means: 'Natural gas is hemispheric. I like to call it hemispheric in nature because it is a product that we can find in our neighbourhoods.'

7. A hummingbird. (PLUS 2)

For its size that is, measured in body lengths per second (bps). They do this amazing dive when courting. Jet fighter: 150 bps; Peregrine falcon: 200 bps; Space shuttle: 207 bps; Hummingbird: 385 bps.

8. He invented the letter 'G'. (PLUS 2)

In around 200 BC, according to Plutarch. Latin originally had no letter G at all: the hard 'C', 'K' and 'G' sounds were all represented by 'C'. Ruga was also the first man in recorded history to open a private elementary school.

ATTACH THE CORRECT SURNAME TO THESE GIFTED GEOFFREYS

(Answers on page 98)

1. This Geoffrey was the most prolifically talented comedy producer of his generation and the nicest man you could possibly meet. Sadly missed by us all at QI.

2. This Geoffrey nearly died aged eight when he fell onto some iron spikes. He once famously said: 'I'm glad two sides of the cherry have been put forward.'

3. This Geoffrey is the only footballer in the world to have scored a hat trick in a World Cup Final – one goal with each foot and one with his head.

4. Known as 'the Geoffrey Boycott of gardening', this Geoffrey described rosemary as 'the bowler, batsman, slip fielder and captain of the herbal cricketing world'.

5. This Geoffrey is the only actor to have appeared in all top three of the BFI's 100 Greatest British TV Programmes: Fawlty Towers, Cathy Come Home and Dr Who.

6. This Geoffrey turned down offers to play the first two Doctor Whos, became famous as Catweazle, and later became the oldest Doctor Who ever.

7. This Geoffrey wrote some of the best-loved TV ads. The first British copywriter to earn £100K per year, his surname is advertising industry slang for a six-figure salary.

8. This Geoffrey began climbing rooftops while at Cambridge University. Despite having a leg amputated in the First World War, he went on to scale the Matterhorn in 1928.

9. This Geoffrey is one of only 20 people in the world to have won an Oscar, a Tony and an Emmy - the so-called 'Triple Crown' of show business.

10. This Geoffrey was a diplomat, scrap metal merchant, philosopher, spy, civil servant, courtier, prisoner of war, customs official, Member of Parliament and poet.

11. This Geoffrey once lectured Africans in Swahili, urging loyalty to 'Bwana Kingy George'. Being attacked by him was said to be 'like being savaged by a dead sheep'.

12. This Geoffrey drew all the other Geoffreys. He has been quoted as saying 'Single stick-figures can be just as exciting as 500 flopsy bunnies' and 'A large one, please.'

G's the fifth note in the scale of C major;
GG is a beast, on which you can wager.
GB is our land - and next former Prime Minister;
GM food is abundant, but frankly quite sinister.
GC marks great courage (not always in battle);
GLC was the place where bores went to prattle.
GBH rearranges your face into Gollum's;
GSOH is a must in personal columns.
GI Joes are all trained to follow instructions;
GBP's worth a dollar (after deductions).
GDP tells economists what we can afford;
GNP is the same – plus our earnings abroad.
GDR was a country, decidedly creepy;
GCSEs must never be tackled when sleepy.
GCHQ is in charge of tracking down spies;
GSR may be found when your worst enemy dies.
GWR is a railway (alas great no more);
G20's a forum (Sorry! No poor!).
GTA's not your game if violence offends
GPS has a woman who drives you round bends
GESTAPO were very unlike Sergeant Dixon;
G-strings aren't much better than having no knicks on.
GIB is a rock that's the home of some monkeys;
GQ readers believe that they're what a real hunk is.
GBS won an Oscar for writing 'Pygmalion';
Gina G sang for Britain but's really Australian.
G Spot marks a treasure that's deep in a cavity;
G Force is acceleration, relative to gravity.
G-Plan's retro furniture – not my style, I'll admit;
G&T is quite fizzy (unlike Gin and It);
GSK are the makers of Lucozade and pills;
GTIs are the cars that go faster up hills.
G Whizz! is a cry of surprise or delight;
GMT just keeps going all day and all night.
And let's not forget GATT, GEC, GMC -
But for now,
I must rush,
Toodle-pip,
GTG!

GB Great Britain, Gordon Brown; **GM** Genetically Modified; **GC** George Cross (the highest civilian award for gallantry); **GLC** Greater London Council (the capital's former local government body); **GBH** Grievous Bodily Harm; **GSOH** Good Sense Of Humour; **GI** Galvanised Iron*; **GBP** Great Britain Pound (Sterling); **GDP** Gross Domestic Product; **GNP** Gross National Product; **GDR** German Democratic Republic (the communist former East Germany); **GCSE** General Certificate of Secondary Education; **GCHQ** Government Communications Headquarters; **GSR** Gun Shot Residue; **GWR** Great Western Railway; **G20** Group (of finance ministers and heads of national banks of the world's) 20 (richest economies); **GTA** Grand Theft Auto; **GPS** Global Positioning System; **GESTAPO GE**heime **STA**ats **PO**lizei (Secret State Police); **GQ** Gentlemen's Quarterly; **GBS** George Bernard Shaw; **G Spot** Gräfenberg spot**; **GSK** GlaxoSmithKline; **GTI** Gran Turismo Injection; **GMT** Greenwich Mean Time; **GATT** General Agreement on Tariffs and Trade (UN agency); **GEC** General Electric Company; **GMC** General Medical Council; **GTG** Got To Go.

*GI (meaning a private soldier in the US army) is sometimes incorrectly said to stand for 'General Infantry', but in fact it has never meant that. The initials were originally used on government inventories to signify equipment made of galvanized iron. This was assumed (again incorrectly) to mean 'Government Issue', and thus applied to anything to do with the army. This stuck and was then adopted officially. So 'Government Issue' is another possible meaning of GI.

**The supposed (and possibly mythical) erogenous zone is named after German gynaecologist Ernst Gräfenberg (1881-1957), who theorised its existence in 1950.

The **QI** Annual was researched, written, illustrated, photographed and otherwise enhanced by Clive Anderson, Rowan Atkinson, Bill Bailey, Jacqueline Bisset, Craig Brown, Stevyn Colgan, Mat Coward, Jonathan Cusick, Cherry Denman, Ted Dewan, Chris Donald, Geoff Dunbar, Hunt Emerson, Arron Ferster, Piers Fletcher, Nadia Flower, Stephen Fry, James Harkin, Andy Hollingworth, Tony Husband, Gray Jolliffe, Phill Jupitus, Roger Law, John Lloyd, Sean Lock, Laura Maddison, Jim Marks, Andy Murray, Nick Newman, Graham Norton, Molly Oldfield, Justin Pollard, Matt Pritchett, Brian Ritchie, Katie Scott, Adrian Teal and Robert Thompson.

The **QI** Annual features Stephen Fry, Alan Davies and the guest panellists from the QI TV 'G' series: Ronni Ancona, Clive Anderson, Bill Bailey, Danny Baker, Jo Brand, Rob Brydon, Jimmy Carr, Jeremy Clarkson, Jack Dee, Hugh Dennis, Rich Hall, Andy Hamilton, Barry Humphries, Phill Jupitus, Sean Lock, Lee Mack, David Mitchell, Graham Norton, Dara O'Briain, Sue Perkins, Jan Ravens, Liza Tarbuck, David Tennant, Sandi Toksvig and Johnny Vegas.

Designed by David Costa (david@whereforeart.com)
Cover illustration: Jonathan Cusick (www.jonathancusick.com)

Editorial: Sarah Lloyd.
Editorial Administrator: Liz Townsend.

Picture Research: Liz Townsend and David Costa.

Photography by: Andy Hollingworth (andyhollingworth@me.com) with assistant Matthew Evered for 'The Gambler'; Andy Hollingworth with Moira Chapman as stylist for 'Bill Bailey's Air Guitar Masterclass'; Jim Marks (www.marks.co.uk) for 'Five Go Gallivanting After Ghosts'; Brian Ritchie (brian@brianjritchie.com) for the **QI** production photographs; photographs of the guinea pig in 'Are You A Guinea Genius' and 'Glee' taken by Kate Kessling (www.contrarypress.com)

The **QI** researchers and writers were: Mat Coward; Arron Ferster; Piers Fletcher; James Harkin; John Lloyd; Laura Maddison; John Mitchinson; Andy Murray; Molly Oldfield and Justin Pollard.

QI Logo design: Jules Bailey

With special thanks to Nicholas Johnston and Jo Jakemen of the Great Tew Estate for allowing us access to Tew Park; Caitlin Lloyd for the loan of 'Guin'; and Dinah Howland for the loan of her Tarot collection.

PHOTO CREDITS: Bigstockphotos (www.bigstockphoto.com) for bullet holes in 'Gallery of Goons'; 'Goatherd', except Mr Mountain Goat image from 'The Mountain and the Molehill', Normalsville Books, provided courtesy of Frank Newman and Pursuit Publishing (NZ) Ltd (www.pursuit.co.nz); silhouette background in 'Golf' and 'I Spy Gravel' pictures, except Justin Pollard for 'Gravel Collection'; Michael Davis, Clearwater, Florida, USA for pay dirt; bybee.com for Sisyphus; Mediscan for kidney stone, and Piedmont Gravel and Bench Gravel which were reproduced by permission of the British Geological Survey © NERC. All rights reserved. IPR/117-46CT. Mary Evans Picture Library for title page images; backgrounds 'Gee-Kwiz' and 'Gee-Kwiz Answers' and featured Gooseberry and Orrery; 'Geese' except feather & inkwell and white goose, courtesy of Getty Images. Getty Images for giraffe skin in 'Giraffes'; 'Gee-Kwiz Answers' and 'Guinea Genius', 'Gielguddies'; and the featured photos in 'Golf' except Arikikapakapa, courtesy of Paul Fowler (www.paulfowler.co.nz). NASA for 'Galaxies'.

THE ANSWER TO THE **QI** SUDO–N'KO IS AVAILABLE FROM WWW.QI.COM

ANSWERS TO 'GUESS THE GEOFF' (P96):
1. *Geoffrey Perkins (1953-2008)*
2. *Geoffrey Boycott, OBE (1940-)*
3. *Sir Geoffrey 'Geoff' Hurst, MBE (1941-)*
4. *Geoffrey Smith (1928-2009)*
5. *Geoffrey Palmer, OBE (1927-)*
6. *Geoffrey Bayldon (1924-)*
7. *Geoffrey Seymour (1947-2008)*
8. *Geoffrey Winthrop-Young (1876 -1958)*
9. *Geoffrey Rush (1951-)*
10. *Geoffrey Chaucer (1343-1400)*
11. *The Rt Hon. The Lord (Geoffrey) Howe of Aberavon, CH, PC, QC (1926-)*
12. *Geoffrey 'Geoff' Dunbar (1944-)*

ANSWERS TO 'GOATWORD' (P93)

Waiting for Mrs Godot